KT-165-534

Stephanie Garrett

GENDER

THE LIBRARY
COLLEGE OF RIPON AND YORK ST. JOHN
COLLEGE ROAD, RIPON HG4 2QX

ROUTLEDGE

London and New York

For Michael and Jonathan

First published in 1987 by
Tavistock Publications Ltd

Reprinted 1992
by Routledge
11 New Fetter Lane,
London EC4P 4EE

29 West 35th Street
New York NY 10001

© 1987 Stephanie Garrett

Typeset by Hope Services,
Abingdon, Oxfordshire
Printed in Great Britain by
Richard Clay, The Chaucer Press
Bungay, Suffolk

All rights reserved. No part of this
book may be reprinted or
reproduced or utilized in any form
or by any electronic, mechanical,
or other means, now known or
hereafter invented, including
photocopying and recording, or in
any information storage or
retrieval system, without
permission in writing from the
publishers.

*British Library Cataloguing
in Publication Data*
Garrett, Stephanie
Gender.—(Society now)
1. Sex role
I. Title II. Series
305.3   BF692.2
ISBN 0-415-08401-6

WITHDRAWN

General Editor:
Patrick McNeill

SOCIETY
NOW

GE OF

Gender

128223

College of Ripon & York St John

3 8025 00316929 2

Other books in the Society Now series

Contents

Acknowledgements

This book is based on some of the themes I have been using in sociology teaching in recent years. I would like to thank the series editor, Pat McNeill, for his encouragement in helping me to write it, and also my students for their comments and ideas.

The author and publishers would like to thank the following for their kind permission to reproduce copyright material: Alan Lerner for the song from *My Fair Lady*, John Wiley & Sons, Inc. for a table from *Gender, An Ethnomethodological Approach*, copyright © 1978 S. Kessler and W. McKenna; Basil Blackwell for *Tables* 2 and 3.

Introduction

Whether you are born male or female will be of major consequence for all aspects of your life: for the expectations others in society will have of you, for your treatment by other people, and for your own behaviour. This is true no matter what society someone is born into, although the consequences will vary from society to society. Virtually all societies are organized on the basis of gender differences between men and women.

Sociologists make an important distinction between 'sex' and 'gender'. The term 'sex' refers to the biological differences between males and females, while 'gender' refers to the socially-determined personal, and psychological characteristics associated with being male or female, namely 'masculinity' and 'femininity'. 'Sex' and 'gender' are clearly related, although the exact nature of this relationship is the subject of much debate among sociologists and others. This book starts with a discussion of the extent of biological sex differences in males and females and of the nature of sexuality. It continues with a chapter on socialization, which explores the ways in which gender differences are learned. This theme continues in the chapters on the family and education. A major argument of this book, and of much recent research, is that gender differences are largely learned, rather than inherited. The remainder of the book considers the significance of gender for the areas of work, politics, deviance, and crime.

Throughout the book I have tried to show that sociologists disagree about explanations for different patterns of gender role behaviour. This is as true of feminist sociologists as of sociologists as a whole. Much of the research discussed in this book is from feminists, whose work in recent years has created a new awareness of the significance of gender in all societies. Broadly, the term 'feminist' describes anyone who argues that women should be recognized as individuals in their own right, and who refuses to take for granted that differences between men and women are *natural*. Feminist sociology can be seen as a reaction to male domination in a subject, which has meant that women's lives have usually been ignored by sociologists unless the area under consideration was the family (in which case the role of men was omitted!). Feminists, however, are not a united group in more than a broad sense, and offer different, sometimes conflicting explanations for what they see as women's oppression. Radical feminists tend to explain women's oppression in terms of male domination while socialist feminists account for it in terms of capitalism. Liberal feminists maintain that solutions for women can be found within existing social structures – a position which would not be shared by radical or socialist feminists.

A number of the activities suggested in the book invite you to carry out what is often referred to as 'content analysis'. There is a set of instructions on page 155 which you might find useful with these exercises.

1

Biology and gender

Many people today believe that biological factors are very influential in shaping the gender roles of men and women in society. It is often argued that men are stronger than women and are therefore better suited to physically exacting work, such as labouring or hunting. Some people maintain that biological factors are responsible for personality and temperamental differences between the sexes and thus women are widely considered to be more emotional than men and to have an innate desire to nurture or care for others. These qualities suit women to such work as nursing, teaching, and caring for children. The qualities women 'naturally' possess are often thought to be inferior, as in the words of this song from *My Fair Lady*, the musical version of Shaw's play *Pygmalion*:

> 'Women are irrational, that's all there is to that!
> Their heads are full of cotton, hay and rags!
> They're nothing but exasperating, irritating, vacillating,
>   calculating, agitating, maddening and infuriating hags!

Why can't a woman be more like a man?
Men are so honest, so thoroughly square;
Eternally noble, historically fair;
Who, when you win, will always give your back a pat!
Why can't a woman be like that?'

A large number of people believe that there are clear cut biological differences between men and women, and that these differences, rather than any cultural values learned during socialization, determine the social roles of men and women. In recent years feminists and others have attacked the notion that biological sex differences are clear cut, and also the view that biology, rather than culture, determines social behaviour.

Biological sex differences

One clear difference between the sexes is that women bear children while men cannot. Males and females also differ in terms of chromosomes, hormones, brain size, and secondary sexual characteristics. For example, the cells of the female ovary contain only the X sex-determining chromosome, while male sperm carry the X or Y chromosome (these chromosomes are so called because of their shape). If after fertilization an embryo has the sex determination XY it will be male, and if it has the XX determination it will be female. During pregnancy embryos develop specifically male or female anatomical forms, with hormones triggered by the chromosomes playing a major part in this process. The word 'hormones' refers to the secretions of the pituitary, adrenal, and thyroid glands as well as the pancreas, ovary, and testis. The number and range of hormones produced by males and females are very similar, but 'normal' [average] women usually produce more oestrogen and progesterone (female sex hormones), while males produce more testosterone and androgens (male sex hormones). At puberty, the production of these hormones increases significantly, leading to the development of secondary sexual characteristics, such as body hair, and males and females become capable of reproduction. As well as these differences – and this is a summary rather than a detailed account – biological maleness is equated with greater size, weight, and strength. At birth the average male baby is heavier and longer than the average female baby. The average female brain is also smaller than the average male brain.

The significance of biological sex differences

As the above description suggests, biological males and females are often presented as two quite distinct categories. Biological factors have been used to explain the different social roles and behaviour of the sexes, and in some instances, as a justification for treating men and women differently. For example, the smaller size of a woman's brain has been said to indicate intellectual inferiority compared to men, and this view has then been used to justify more favourable treatment and better opportunities for men in education. Clarke (1873), quoted in Best and Birke (1980), considered education undesirable for women because it would seriously impair their capacity to bear children – the latter being their primary purpose in life. Women's hormones have been used to explain their lack of intellectual achievement and 'irrational' behaviour. Dalton (1979) has maintained that, in the week preceding menstruation, when female hormones undergo considerable fluctuation, women achieve poorer results in academic work, and are more likely than at other times to beat their children, commit crime, attempt suicide, and acquire viral infections. She presents women's behaviour as determined by biology. In addition to the above, Dalton claims that women are subject to 'pre-menstrual tension', for which the symptoms include depression, tearfulness, tiredness, weight gain, and irritability. It is a time when they are emotionally unstable, and there is little they can do about it. Those who argue that women are temperamentally distinct from men and that the differences are biologically based have argued that they should be excluded

3

from certain forms of work because their emotional instability makes them unable to cope with responsibility and stress.

In many cultures the fact that women menstruate has been used to justify their exclusion from social activities, and such taboos still operate in some societies today. In the majority of human societies menstruating women are feared or considered dangerous, and are expected to keep their menstruation a closely-guarded secret. One of the few exceptions to this, according to Best and Birke (1980), is the society of the Congo Pygmies, where menstrual blood is associated with life. This is another example of the way in which biological differences are used to legitimate social differences between the sexes.

Activity

Interview some women who are housewives and mothers at home in order to find out what the *physical* demands of the job are. Find out, for example, what kinds of weight they carry around (children, shopping), how much bending and stretching etc. is required to do housework? Interview some men of the same general age as the women – possibly their partners – to find out what work they do and how much physical strength is involved in their job, bearing in mind differences between white collar and blue collar jobs.

Do your results justify the popular view of women as the 'weaker' sex? If not, why do you think this view of women persists?

Women in many cultures are regarded as the 'weaker' sex, not only because of their lack of physical strength, but also because they are more often unwell than men. Their biology, rather than any other factor, is considered responsible for this. Statistics for Britain seem to confirm this view of women:

one in six women, as opposed to one in nine men, may expect to spend some time in a psychiatric hospital during their lives, while women will visit their general practitioner more often than men. Statistics for illness rates have shown that the rates for women are consistently and substantially higher than those for men, according to Standing, quoted in Best and Birke (1980). A number of anthropological studies show that in many societies, such as the Zulu and the Hausa, illness is explicitly associated with women. The Hausa maintain that 'only women can become ill'.

Biological sex differences in sociological theory

In sociology, biological sex differences have been used to explain and to legitimate a sexual division of labour within the family and in society as a whole. Tiger and Fox (1972) argue that men and women have different 'biogrammars', or genetically-based programmes, which predispose them to behave in distinct ways. The male biogrammar predisposes men to be aggressive and dominant, while the female biogrammar predisposes women to have children and to care for them. The biogrammar thus explains and justifies men's dominance of societal decision-making and politics, and female domination of childcare. The biogrammars that men and women have today are inherited from their ancestors who lived in hunting and gathering societies. Male and female biogrammars are not absolutely fixed, but they change very slowly, and change cannot be brought about by what Tiger and Fox see as the 'unnatural' attempts of either sex to challenge existing roles. Murdock (1949) found that in a study of 224 societies men were predominantly responsible for physically-demanding tasks like hunting and mining, while women were responsible for domestic tasks and childcare. He explained this division of labour not in terms of the biogrammar, but in terms of men's greater physical strength, which was genetically based, and in terms of women's role in reproduction. These biological differences constituted a practical basis for a sexual divison of labour in society as a whole – a division that Murdock, like Tiger and Fox, saw as wholly 'natural' and wholly desirable from both society's point of view and from that of individual men and women.

Parsons (1959) maintains that women have an instinct to nurture as a result of their biologically-based role in reproduction, and this makes them ideally suited for an 'expressive' role in the nuclear family. An 'expressive' role involves caring for the physical and emotional needs of all family members, particularly those of dependent children. Male biology suits men to the 'instrumental' role in the family, involving the provision of economic support and links with the world outside the family. If a human baby is to develop into a stable adult capable of taking its place in society it must, according to Parsons, be socialized in a family where the adults play these two roles. A sexual division of labour in the family is thus seen as essential to ensure 'normal' development. Parsons thought that the socialization function of the family was a crucial factor in the maintenance of social stability, and that no institution could carry out this function as well as the family. The work of such psychologists as Bowlby (1953) and Winnicott (1944), both of whom argued that the constant presence of the woman in a mothering role was an essential factor in the production of non-delinquent, stable adults, supports the notion of a sexual division of labour in the family and in society as a whole. Any activity which takes women out of the family and away from their children is implicitly condemned as 'unnatural'.

Politicians as well as sociologists have presented a sexual division of labour in the family and society as 'natural' and desirable. In 1979 the then Conservative minister, Patrick Jenkin, stated in a BBC 'Man Alive' documentary: 'If the good Lord had intended us all having equal rights to go out to work and behave equally, you know he really wouldn't have created man and woman . . . these are the biological facts of life, that young children do depend on their mothers.' The view that there is a biologically-based maternal instinct is one that is shared by many 'experts' in childcare, such as Spock, Leach, and Jolly, all of whom disapprove of women who appear not to behave in accordance with it. It is also the view of many health professionals, and strongly influenced welfare state legislation introduced in Britain in 1945. Hunt (1975) found that many employers used biology as a justification for treating women differently from men as workers. She discovered that women were widely regarded as less desirable employees than men because they were believed to be more prone to illness and therefore more likely to be absent from work than men, and also because they were all seen as potential mothers. Pregnancy meant time away from work, as did children. Men were seen as healthier, more ambitious, and more committed to work than women. One advantage of women workers, from the point of view of many employers in the past and possibly the present, is their 'natural' docility. They have been seen as less likely to take industrial action and able to cope very well with repetitive, monotonous work.

Feminist responses

Feminists have reacted strongly to the views of women and men described in the previous sections. They maintain that 'biological essentialism', or the idea that men and women are determined by biology, is not proven, and that as an idea it is inimical to men's and women's interests as individuals.

Feminists have challenged the notion that men and women are two separate, distinct biological categories. Oakley (1972, 1981) provides a comprehensive account of the work done in this field. She suggests that 'male' and 'female' should be viewed as categories at opposing ends of a continuum, with considerable overlapping in the middle. There is great variation in the biological characteristics of males and females, and such characteristics as great height, weight, and physical strength are not confined to just one category. Some

7

individuals, such as those studied by Money and Ehrhardt (1972), are born with both 'male' and 'female' characteristics such as male genitalia and female reproductive organs. These individuals usually undergo surgery and cortisone therapy in order to be assigned to the category 'female'. They would be in the centre of the proposed continuum.

Oakley's discussion suggests that the hormonal differences between men and women are by no means as clear or as great as is often assumed. Males and females have the same sex hormones present in their bodies but in different quantities. The function of sex hormones is to ensure that the body develops in line with chromosomal sex and becomes capable of reproduction. However, the output of the male sex hormone testosterone varies between males so that not all males are equally hairy. (This hormone encourages the growth of body hair at puberty.) Some females have more testosterone than others and therefore more body hair, although this is not obvious in the western world because of the female custom of shaving.

Feminists have questioned the view that the behaviour and temperament of women are determined by their hormones. They do not accept the view that the hormonal changes associated with menstruation are responsible for women allegedly behaving more emotionally, or being unable to cope with work at this time. Oakley maintains that there is as yet no proof of a biochemical connection between changing emotional conditions and the physiological changes accompanying the menstrual cycle. Best and Birke (1980) argue that, although for many women changes of mood during the menstrual cycle *are* a reality, this does not mean that such changes are directly dependent on hormones. The existence in most societies of a strong taboo relating to menstruation, plus the anticipation of discomfort, may for many women be sufficient to create the symptoms noted by Dalton and others and indeed make these symptoms much worse than they might otherwise be. Women from other cultures report different symptoms from those noted by Dalton in the pre-menstrual and menstrual phases, suggesting that the experience of menstruation is influenced by cultural values.

Best and Birke (1980) maintain that there is evidence that intellectual performance does not vary significantly during the menstrual cycle. They suggest that because of the value placed on constant, unvarying behaviour by our culture, any *changes* reported by women during menstruation are automatically seen as negative, regardless of whether or not the woman herself experiences them in this way. 'It seems that the very fact of change is seen as undesirable, that we are judged by the ideal of the supposedly-constant male and found wanting. We must ask ourselves the question: to whom are these changes undesirable?' They argue that feminists must refuse to accept scientists' negative evaluation of female cycles and instead should learn to evaluate these changes positively. Science has for too long been used to legitimate the notion that women are inferior because of their biology, and women have for too long accepted uncritically scientific studies of female biology which are incomplete and far from thorough.

Oakley (1972) quotes a number of pieces of research that in fact demonstrate that men as well as women are subject to monthly cycles and changes in mood. Persky (1974) tested the moods of twenty-nine women at three points in the menstrual cycle and compared them with those of a male control group. He found that the results for both sexes were similar. Work like this supports the notion of the similarity or overlap between 'male' and 'female' categories rather than the notion of difference.

The role of science in establishing sex differences

Oakley argues that attempts to measure biological sex differences have inevitably stressed the differences rather than the similarities between males and females. Many feminists point to the fact that male scientists have been responsible for most of this work. They claim that men have deliberately sought to provide scientific support for the view that the two

9

sexes are separate biological categories, that the qualities associated with the male are superior and that social behaviour is determined by biology, because such 'evidence' justifies men occupying powerful and prestigious positions in society. The Brighton Women and Science Group write: 'The role of science in confirming women's oppression is not new.' Nineteenth-century scientists, for example, suggested that women were less evolved than men; that their reproductive function drew vital energy from their brains, implying that their intellectual development was retarded and that by nature they were weak and frail. Medical journals in the 1870s warned of the terrible consequences for women if they tried to reject their reproductive role by using contraception or entering higher education. These consequences included 'death or severe illness . . . leucorrhoea, menorrhagia, cancer, mania leading to suicide, and repulsive nymphomania'. Such 'scientific' evidence was used by those who supported the anti-female suffrage movement in Britain. This evidence, argue such feminists as Wallsgrove (1980), legitimates the inferior position of women in society because it is based on the idea that, since women's position is due to biological inferiority, there is little point in trying to change that position.

Feminists have drawn attention to the fact that much research on the subject of sex differences is based on animal studies. This, they maintain, means that the research is fundamentally flawed, because it fails to recognize that human beings and animals are qualitatively different – for example, in terms of their ability to learn and to manipulate the environment. Findings from animal studies cannot legitimately be applied to humans, nor is it legitimate to suggest, as does Morris (1967) that human beings are merely a sophisticated type of animal.

Wallsgrove (1980) and others argue that most of us are not accustomed to taking a critical view of science or scientists. We have probably never regarded science or scientists as anything other than 'objective'. Feminists maintain that science is a male-dominated activity which has been used to legitimate gender divisions in society. It is most certainly not the objective activity many of us believe it to be: 'Science is not all logical – it proceeds by intuition and analogy – scientists are emotionally involved with their work'.

Cross-cultural evidence

The view that male and female behaviour is determined by universal biological factors or instincts is challenged by evidence on gender roles from many different societies showing tremendous variation in these roles. Oakley (1972) is critical of Murdock's claim to have found no evidence of cultural variation. Looking at the same societies that Murdock studied, she concludes that there are rules in every society about which activities are 'suitable' for men and women, but that these rules vary considerably and do not support any generalizations about the influence of biological factors on behaviour. The anthropologist Evans-Pritchard argues that Murdock's work is characterized by poor sampling, arbitrary, and inadequate criteria of classification and an 'almost unbelievably uncritical use of sources'.

Evidence of different patterns of parenting is discussed (see pages 51–6), and of work (see pages 95–9). The work of Mead (1935) is a well-known example of anthropological research showing cultural variation in gender roles. She studied the variation in masculine and feminine personality types in three New Guinea tribes, the Arapesh, Mundugumor, and Tchambuli. The 'ideal adult' among the Arapesh was gentle, caring, and passive – characteristics that, in terms of British culture, would be regarded as 'feminine'. In sexual relationships neither adult was regarded as the initiator. Both parents were described as 'bearing children' and both cared for them. Among the Mundugumor, males and females alike were assertive and hostile to the opposite sex. Women detested pregnancy and childcare. Among the Tchambuli, men were typically interested in art, the theatre, and gossip –

they were often jealous of one another – while women were practical, self-assertive, and dominating. Tchambuli men, but not women, were very interested in their own physical appearance.

The conclusions Mead drew about life in another society, Samoa, have recently been questioned by the anthropologist Freeman (1983). Mead presented Samoan people as peace-loving and saw Samoan culture as the chief determinant of social behaviour. However, she spent only nine months in the society; she did not learn the language and did not live among the people but in a compound with other westerners. Freeman, who spent five years doing research in the same society, argues that, as a result, her portrait of Samoan society is inaccurate. Freeman questions how valid Mead's picture of New Guinea was, influenced no doubt by his apparent assumption that biology is the most powerful determinant of human behaviour.

Mead's work suggests that other cultures do not always make a strict distinction between men and women. This is also shown by the work of Turnbull (1965) on the Mbuti pygmies. Here both sexes take part in hunting, gathering, and childcare – a fact reflected in their language, which contains no words for 'girl' or 'boy', referring only to 'child'. There are examples of cultures where a much more rigid distinction is made between the sexes than in western culture. The Mundurucu Indians in Brazil separate men and women both physically and socially. Men and boys live in men's houses separate from all females, and each sex group, with the exception of very young children, interacts only with itself. Within this culture both men and women demonstrate great concern to stay within the prescribed gender roles and anxiety about this and any real or imaginary wish to transcend them is shown in many pieces of folklore and ritual.

Such characteristics as physical strength and aggression are not confined to males, according to many studies. Levi Strauss has shown that women are active as fighters and soldiers in a number of cultures, not all of which are non-industrial.

12

Many feminists maintain that physical strength is a quality that develops during socialization rather than being innate. They argue that in western societies males receive much more encouragement than females to be physically active and adventurous, which leads to their developing this quality. Similarly, women's 'natural' preoccupation with their appearance is the result of socialization in western societies, as is their 'natural' concern with caring for children. It is the wealth of evidence from cross-cultural studies that makes their argument very convincing.

Sexuality – popular assumptions

Sexuality has been an area of particular interest to feminists in recent years, and their work has challenged ideas that are often taken for granted in western societies. Many people assume that, because of biological differences, men's and women's experience of sex, their needs for it, and their attitudes towards it will also be different. Men, for example, are believed to have a strong need for sexual intercourse which is biologically based and in relationships they are motivated by physical desire rather than by emotional feelings. Men's 'natural' promiscuity has been used to justify prostitution, extra-marital affairs, and even rape. Men are thought of as the initiators of sexual relationships whereas women are believed to be passive by nature and more interested in the overall relationship with their partner, rather than in the physical side. Women respond to sexual advances; they do not make them.

Such views of male and female sexuality have been expressed by academics as 'scientific'. Freud, for instance, portrayed female sexuality as passive and subordinate. In a textbook on the physiology of sex Walker (1954) writes: 'What we may term sexual hunger or the dynamic drive of one sex towards the other is stronger in the male than in the female' while Barnes (1970) writes: 'I think it would be fair to say that until she is married and deeply roused by all that marriage means, the desire for sexual intercourse is not very strong in a girl.' A Department of Education and Science report on health education stated in 1977 'Girls should understand that they may inadvertently impose great stress on boys by arousing sexual reactions in them which they do not fully comprehend and may not be able to control.'

Popular assumptions and work such as that described above accepts the idea of a basic and 'natural' sexual difference between men and women and also the notion that both sexes are 'naturally' interested in heterosexual relationships. It also legitimates the notion of different norms for men and women in relation to the expression of sexuality. For example, as Adams and Lauriekitis (1976) point out, men are expected to show an interest in women's bodies; this is one way for a man in our society to prove that he's 'normal'. Men are expected to initiate relationships that might involve sex, and a man who has many sexual conquests among women is regarded as 'a real male'. Women are expected to be passive and non-promiscuous. A sexually-active woman often receives social disapproval and often a negative label such as 'slag', 'whore', or 'tramp'. Cowie and Lees (1983) have shown that it is not merely sexual promiscuity that gets a girl a 'bad reputation'; it may simply be any behaviour on the part of the girl that indicates a direct interest in boys or sex, such as dressing in what is regarded as a 'sexy' manner, or hanging around boys too much. The existence of a 'double standard' means that men are allowed to express their sexuality more openly than women and to behave in ways which, in women, would be condemned. However, there is condemnation for both men and women who show an interest in homosexual, rather than in heterosexual relationships. Such individuals are often the objects of ridicule, disapproval, and discrimination. Despite the legalization of homosexual acts between consenting males over the age of twenty-one in our society and the gay liberation movement of the sixties, many homosexuals still fear the consequences of revealing their sexuality, of 'coming

14

out'. Because there is still so much prejudice they fear losing their job or their friends.

The view that sexuality is biologically based, and that male sexuality is more aggressive than female sexuality, is accepted by some radical feminists, including Brownmiller (1975). Radical feminists explain women's oppression in terms of men, as opposed to liberal and socialist feminists who explain women's oppression in terms of socialization and the economic and cultural exploitation of capitalism respectively. Brownmiller maintains that male power over women in society is symbolized by an act of extreme violence such as rape (see page 150). The transformation of sexuality is thus a major priority for all women – they should have control over their own sexuality. For some radical feminists this means ending sexual relations with men – and only when this occurs will male domination be challenged. Socialist and liberal feminists do not accept such an 'essentialist' view of biology and sexuality (see page 7), nor the recommendations of radical feminists.

Some feminist research on sexuality

McIntosh (1978) argues that there is little evidence to support popular assumptions about male and female sexuality, but shows that such assumptions are often implicit in analyses of such areas as prostitution and rape. Female prostitutes are often seen as catering for the sexual needs of unfulfilled, unattractive, and single men, but there is no parallel need for male prostitutes by women because, it is implied, women are satisfied with less sex. Some writers, she claims, express surprise that women prostitutes engage in casual sex, but rarely is any surprise expressed about the fact that their male clients do this. This demonstrates the view that women are only satisfied with sex in the context of a relationship whereas to men it is the act of sex itself that is important. Weeks (1981), in his analysis of changing norms relating to sexuality, believes that the desire to preserve the institution of the family

15

in capitalist societies led to a denial of female sexuality in capitalist culture. In such societies women are defined primarily as wives and mothers – firmly within the family – while male promiscuity is accepted because it poses no threat to the institution of the family.

Feminists use evidence from other cultures and historical periods to support their argument that both male and female sexuality are heavily influenced by culture. This position does not involve a total rejection of biology exercising some influence on sexuality, but it decisively rejects the notion that there are universal patterns of sexual behaviour. Oakley (1972) writes: 'Anthropology shows that the whole area of human sexuality is subject to tremendous cultural variation.' She lists the following features of human sexual behaviour that have been found to vary: sexual play between children (which may be specifically genital and widely encouraged throughout childhood, as among the Trobriand islanders, or heavily discouraged as in many western societies), intercourse between immature adults (which, as in Samoa, may be a common occurrence, not tied to marriage or reproduction – or discouraged, as in our own society), the emphasis placed on sexual activity itself (which among the Truk is more important than any other activity, but which is quite unimportant to the Arapesh), the extent to which sexual desire is considered dangerous and in need of control, as among the Manus, or as weak and likely to fail, as in Bali. The idea that male and female sexuality are very different is not universal, as shown by Davenport's study of a South West Pacific society (1965), where intercourse was considered highly enjoyable for both sexes. In this culture it was believed that a lack of intercourse was harmful for both men and women. Young married couples had intercourse at least twice a day, and it was legitimate for either husband or wife to end a marriage if intercourse was not frequent enough – after a gap of ten days. After puberty and before marriage both sexes were encouraged to masturbate and it was believed that, given appropriate stimulation, neither sex could fail to reach orgasm. Amongst the Trobrianders, Lesu, Kurtachi, Lepcha, Kwoma, and Matuco, women frequently initiate sexual relationships and intercourse; in the last two societies women alone do this.

Henry (1964), in his account of the life of a tribe in the Brazilian highlands, describes the total lack of emphasis on temperamental differences between the sexes in this culture. Jocular and robust sexual aggressiveness – acceptable only in men in western societies – is displayed by both sexes. Men and women in this tribe make 'open, ribald, and aggressive onslaughts', including some by women on Henry himself. Other societies have different expectations relating to the expression of sexuality without there being a total reversal of western stereotypes. In Iran, a patriarchal society, women are nevertheless expected to be cool, calm, and calculating, while men are expected to display emotion, sensitivity, and intuition.

Oakley writes that evidence on sexuality from non-western cultures is frequently dismissed as deviant, eccentric, or irrelevant to the mainstream of human development. She describes this reaction as 'absurdly ethnocentric'. The history of western culture, she argues, contains within it exactly the same type of reversal or semi-reversal of current popular assumptions about male and female sexuality. In Anglo-Saxon times women were self-assertive and independent like many African women today. According to the historian Garreau, there existed in France at the time of the crusades 'a close resemblance between the manners of men and women'. Oakley, and Sayers (1982) are highly critical of the way in which some writers base their conclusions about human sexuality on animal studies. The males of non-human species used to provide comparisons (these were often chimpanzees) are dominant, sexually aggressive, and show no desire to give pleasure to the female; while the non-human females have no alternatives to constant procreation and nursing. Oakley writes: 'This [analogy] is absurd in its application to human culture, enabling the patriarchal world to be supported in its

17

very foundations, justifying the aggressive acts of the male in the bedroom by reference to the jungle and providing a rationale for aggressive acts [in other areas of social life]'.

The role of culture in shaping sexuality

Many feminists argue that sexuality is shaped by culture and socialization and have drawn attention to some of the most important aspects of this in western societies. Parents play a crucial part in the process of socialization (see page 53). In western cultures parents' expectations of appropriate behaviour in teenage girls often exclude overt sexual activity, whereas for boys it is permitted or overlooked. This is indicated by Schofield's study (1965) of the sexual behaviour of young people. He found that girls were far more closely controlled by the family than boys and as a result, had far fewer opportunities than boys to gain sexual experience. Girls were also more emotionally involved with their families than boys and placed a higher value on conforming to parental wishes than boys. The 'average' boy was more sexually experienced than the 'average' girl as a result. In order for a girl to reach a similar level of experience as the 'average' boy, she would have had to positively reject parental influence. This would mean that she would refuse to provide information to her parents about where she was going, who she was going out with, or when she would be back; she would spend most of her leisure time out of the home rather than in it, and she would refuse advice on boyfriends and sexual matters from her parents.

Definitions of 'appropriate' sexual behaviour are communicated to boys and girls through the education system as well as the family, via both the 'official' and the 'hidden' curriculum (page 181). Sex education now features on the curricula of most schools, but such lessons, argues Rance (1982), mostly reinforce 'traditional' definitions of sexuality. Female sexuality is almost always presented as reproductive (about having babies rather than pleasure) and submissive. In a recent (1977) paper on health education, the DES itself accepted the notion of males having a more powerful and less controllable sex drive than females. Wolpe (1977) found that stereotyped definitions of sexuality were accepted by teachers at the secondary school she studied. Girls who flirted with male teachers, and who behaved in a coquettish manner, were often favoured by these teachers and given more friendly attention, while in the same school, girls who complained about male students groping them in the corridors at break-times were told that this was just the 'natural' high spirits of the boys: in other words, their complaints were not taken seriously.

Further reading

Adams and Lauriekitis (1976) Volume 2 provides a non-technical discussion of the topic of sexuality. Oakley (1972) has a chapter summarizing research on sexuality, sex and intelligence, sex and personality and biological sex differences. For an explicitly feminist perspective, there is Best and Birke (Brighton Women and Science Group) (1980) or Sayers (1982).

2

The socialization of gender roles

Introduction

How do children learn that they are girls or boys? How does gender role behaviour develop as they become adults? What is the influence of specific factors such as parental behaviour and mass media in the process of gender socialization?

At birth, a baby is assigned to the male or female gender on inspection of its genitals, and this profoundly influences its subsequent experiences. She or he develops gender identity, a term referring to an individual's own feelings and consciousness of whether she or he is a woman or man, girl or boy, and learns a gender role – a set of expectations about the behaviour considered appropriate for people of that gender. These expectations vary according to the way in which 'masculinity' and 'femininity' are defined. Unless we accept that the basis for gender is completely biological, it is necessary to refer to social or environmental factors that interact with biological factors and lead to the development of gender identity and gender role. There is, however, considerable disagreement among social scientists about the nature of the socialization, or learning, process, and in relation to the importance of particular factors in this process, as this chapter will show.

Perspectives on gender development

There are three main psychological theories of gender development: *cognitive developmental theory*, *social learning theory*, and *psychoanalytic theory*. These are all concerned with the notion of 'identification', the process through which girls come to identify with the feminine model and boys with the masculine model. However they vary in their assumptions about the age at which gender identity develops, whether gender identity leads to the adoption of a gender role or vice versa, and about the role of parents in the development of both gender identity and gender role.

Cognitive developmental theory

This theory maintains that gender is based on genital sex and is thus a physical property of people that has to be learned in the same way as other unchanging physical properties as for example, that ice is cold. It argues that children see the world in a radically different way from adults, and that their development involves the gradual learning of an adult perspective. Although a child of two or three can label itself accurately as a boy or a girl, it does not know at this age that a person's gender is based on physical factors, nor that a person's gender cannot change. A child of this age does not understand that physical objects have an unchangeable quality and that, for example, boys cannot become girls at will. By the age of six, however, a female child not only knows that she is a girl but that she will always be one. When this realization occurs, she begins to demonstrate a definite preference for activities and behaviour that are defined as 'feminine'. When she adopts such behaviour she is rewarded,

21

for instance, by parental approval. From this point onwards, according to the theory, children develop a conscious wish to be like the same-sex parent and other adults of the same sex.

Social learning theory

This theory argues that the learning of gender roles takes place first through observation, then by imitation. Parents play a crucial role in this process because of the amount of time they spend in close contact with children and because of the emotional relationship children have with them. Parents reward children for behaviour they consider to be gender-appropriate; children learn to anticipate what will produce approval and behave accordingly. Parents and other adults distinguish between males and females in terms of their interaction with them. The child learns the label 'boy' or 'girl' appropriate to the behaviour that is rewarded, learns to apply that label to him or herself, and to positively value the label. According to this theory, gender identity develops after gender role behaviour has been established. It does not occur at a particular age.

Psychoanalytic theory

Based on the work of Freud, this theory maintains that a child's awareness of the differences in boys' and girls' genitals is of crucial importance in the development of gender identity. At first, the development of boys and girls is similar; both focus their love on the person who spends most time with them – the mother. Around the age of five, boys become aware that they have a penis and girls that they do not, and this leads to their developing a fantasy involving their genitals and their parents, as a result of which they come to identify with the same-sex parent. Imitation follows identification, and gender role behaviour develops.

The following table sets out the differences between the three theories:

Table 1 *Theories of Gender Development*

Freudian
psychoanalytic: own awareness of genitals → fantasy → identification → gender role
(implicit: gender identity)

Social
learning: others' awareness of genitals → differential → identification (modeling)
reinforcement → gender role → gender identity

Cognitive
developmental: others' awareness → labeling → gender identity → gender role → identification
of genitals

Source: Kessler and McKenna (1978).

23

Evaluation of gender development theories

Cognitive developmental theory

This theory accounts for the fact that children know their own gender and can describe themselves correctly as boys or girls and choose gender-appropriate toys and activities, before they are able to relate this to genital sex differences. It argues that gender identity happens before the idea takes root in the child's mind that gender is fixed. It claims that while parental behaviour is important, it is probably not the most influential factor. This point is supported by Maccoby and Jacklin's findings (1974) that the activities selected by children at nursery school are frequently at variance with those that their parents have encouraged at home. There are, however, a number of criticisms of the theory. As Maccoby and Jacklin (1974) have argued, children do not need to understand that gender is fixed and permanent in order for 'self-socialization' to begin; for example, three-year-olds show clear gender-typed preferences in toys and games, and the influence of these choices on future behaviour cannot be dismissed. There is some evidence from Money and Ehrhardt (1972) to question the theory's assumption that gender identity is not firmly fixed until the age of five or six. Their work shows that gender identity is firmly fixed in the first two years of life, in more or less the same period as native language is established. After this point, for those individuals whose gender has been incorrectly assigned because of some physical ambiguity (such as children born with internal female organs but with masculinized genitals), gender re-assignment is not usually successful.

Social learning theory

This theory does not concern itself with the origins or content of definitions of 'masculinity' or 'femininity'. It claims that children learn gender identity and gender roles in much the same way that they learn other things. Parents and others, through the giving of rewards and sanctions, encourage children to adopt what they consider to be the appropriate gender role; indeed, the assumption that parents clearly differentiate between boys and girls is central to this theory. There are, however, contradictory findings from studies on how much parents differentiate between male and female children (see next section on 'parents'). Kessler and McKenna (1982) state that social learning theory is a useful way of describing the development of gender identity. Even though a daughter may not wear makeup when she is adult, she does learn (because the label is differentially applied), that she is a girl, and that girls are expected to behave differently from boys.

Psychoanalytic theory

Very little recent work has supported this theory's basic assumption that physical sex differences are the most important determinant of gender identity for children. Gender identity is fixed before children are aware of genital differences. Person (1974) found that blind children develop stable gender identities and share social definitions of femininity and masculinity. Money and Ehrhardt (1972) found children with male gender identities but no penis, and children with female gender identities and a penis. Also, contrary to Freud's theory, children continue to learn gender roles throughout life rather than ceasing to develop with the resolution of their childhood fantasy. Recent work has also suggested that identification with a parental model is not the most powerful influence in establishing adult gender identity.

Feminists have criticised all three theories for their concentration on male development, and have pointed out that many of those responsible for the theories are male. This concentration has resulted, according to Kessler and McKenna (1982), in a relative inability to understand how girls develop.

The role of parents in gender socialization

All three theories of gender development argue that parents are a major influence on their children, but there is little agreement about the precise nature of this influence. Questions that have interested researchers are: what role models do parents provide for their children to imitate, observe or identify with; and do parents interact differently with male and female children.

Parental interaction with children

Maccoby and Jacklin (1974) claim that for the most part, children are not treated differently by their parents on the basis of gender. Any differential treatment is limited to parents providing gender-typed clothes and toys, especially for boys. Other studies have produced a considerable amount of evidence disagreeing with this claim. Moss (1970) found that mothers differentiate between boys and girls in their behaviour towards them even when they are new-born babies. Male babies, according to Moss' study, were cuddled for considerably longer periods than females. This might have been due to behaviour differences as the male babies showed greater irritability and cried more. However, even when babies were in the same state (asleep, crying, awake, quiet) the mothers tended to stimulate and arouse the male babies more. Girl babies' noises and actions were repeated back to the baby by the mother more frequently than to the boys. As the babies got older, mothers made less of an effort to soothe the males. Moss sees this as the initiation of a pattern in keeping with cultural expectations according to which males are seen as more assertive and less responsive than females. Murphy (1962) found that mothers appeared to treat male children with respect for their independence; when babies, this meant following the baby's own rhythm and adopting a 'come and get it' approach. Girls were more fussed over than boys. Hartley (1966) found that mothers were much more preoccupied with girls' appearance than with boys' appearance. This led to girls being dressed in 'feminine' clothes and to frequent references to their appearance. Clothing emphasizes the gender of a child (gender-typing of clothes often begins in hospital when babies are born) as do certain colours: blue for boys and pink for girls. Lake (1975) found that the appearance of the same baby in gender-typed clothes produced different responses from a group of ten mothers. He gave five of them Beth, a six-month-old in a pink frilly dress for a period of observed interaction. The other five were given Adam, a six-month-old in blue overalls. Compared to Adam, Beth attracted more smiles, was offered a doll to play with, and was described as 'sweet' with a 'soft cry'. Beth and Adam were the same baby.

Activity

Analyse a children's clothes catalogue, such as the one from Mothercare shops. Are male and female babies and children shown in different types of clothing and in clothing of different colours? What does this suggest about the activities they are expected to show an interest in? See page 155, *Appendix: Content Analysis*.

Sears, Maccoby, and Levin (1957) found that American mothers distinguished between the kinds of household chores assigned to boys and girls even at five years of age. Girls' work was washing up, bedmaking, and laying the table; boys' work was emptying rubbish, ashtrays, and waste baskets. However, parents were largely unconscious of the fact that this might produce gender-typed behaviour in the children. The different behaviour of male and female children was seen as 'natural' rather than as the product of learning.

27

Toys and games

Oakley (1981) writes that gender differences are probably much more important than class differences in determining what toys children are given. She maintains that gender-appropriate toys are both the cause and proof of 'correct' gender identification. In Britain girls are not usually given guns or soldiers to play with and boys are not normally offered dolls or doll's houses. Goodman (1972) found in an American study that children under two were given very similar presents, for example cuddly toys, building blocks, and rattles, but from then on gender-appropriate toys were selected by buyers (mainly parents). The occasional exception to this rule was made for a highly individual child, for example a girl who liked trains. In the department store where the research was based, Goodman found that more time was spent by buyers in choosing presents for boys rather than for girls. Major influences on buyers were the packaging of toys and advice given by sales assistants. More money was spent on boys' presents, and they were more likely to receive toys and games, whereas girls were more likely to be given clothes or furniture. Goodman argues that girls' toys prepare them for motherhood and domesticity, while boys' toys offer fantasy, excitement, and intellectual stimulation.

Activity

Carry out an analysis of a number of toy catalogues (these are mostly obtainable from toy shops, for example Mothercare, Habitat, Toymaster). Does the text suggest that any toys are specifically for girls or boys? Are girls and boys shown playing with gender-typed toys in the photographs?

Compare your findings for several catalogues (this could be done as a group exercise). How do you react to the way in which toys are shown in these catalogues? See page 155, *Appendix: Content Analysis.*

Children's books and magazines

Recent research suggests that children's literature reinforces traditional gender stereotypes. It refers to the presence of stereotypes, the depiction of a male-dominated world, and the unreal nature of the world of most stories. In fairy tales (for example, Sleeping Beauty and Cinderella) women and girls are presented as dependent and as victims, while the men are romantic heroes or intelligent problem-solvers. Stories usually have men or boys as the main characters.

Activity

Analyse a selection of children's fiction for the under-fives – a good source of material would be a children's library. Do the descriptions above fit the books in your sample? Are there any exceptions? See page 155, *Appendix: Content Analysis*. You might then consider fiction for the five-to-ten age group and compare results.

Children's reading schemes have also been criticised for containing gender stereotypes and for presenting children with an unreal world (see page 70). According to Braman (1977), comics are read by 97 per cent of children. Few of these are written for a mixed-sex readership. Boys' comics centre on interests like sport, football, and fishing, and feature stories about men who are strong, brave, and aggressive. Girls' comics do not centre on interests (with the exception of fashion) but contain stories; Sharpe (1976) writes that the backgrounds to these stories are much narrower than those for boys, and tend to centre on the themes of home, family, or school. The subjects of stories are family conflicts or untrustworthy friends. Walkerdine (1984) found that a constant theme of stories in such comics as *Bunty* and *Tracy* was 'the girl as victim', usually of the dreadful and deliberate

29

treatment by wicked characters, and the typical response to this was passive acceptance. Heroines never show real anger, and a positive girl finds true happiness through self-denial and helping others. Stories of female initiative or deviation from these traditional virtues usually end in disaster for the girl, while those who demonstrate positive virtues are rewarded with a happy home or a romantic hero.

Sharpe (1976) writes that in comics, boys have an exciting array of characters to identify with, such as soldiers, spacemen, cowboys, scientists, or sports stars, but in boys' comics there are very few female characters. Male characters in girls' comics tend to be villains, fathers, or figures of authority, but rarely friends or equals. In boys' comics, male characters are often shown doing things together, but the female characters in girls' comics are often shown as isolated and lonely.

Some comics are aimed at newly-teenage girls, for example *Tina* and *Diana*. These feature stories about pop stars and a few 'boy meets girl' stories. Sharpe (1976) describes them as a childlike 'warm up' to magazines devoted entirely to the pursuit of romance.

Adult books and magazines

Magazines for teenage girls, like *Jackie*, *Oh Boy*, and *My Guy* revolve around boyfriends, love, and romance. Many of the stories are told in photo strips rather than line drawings, which blurs the line between fantasy and reality. In these magazines a particular kind of femininity is endorsed: heterosexual femininity. Women are portrayed as obsessed with finding a man and unable to survive happily without one. However, heroines do not have romances with married men! Careers, serious work, and study are not the main pre-occupations; in fact, these topics are hardly ever mentioned. Feature articles are on fashion and pop stars. Another feature is the problem page, where advice is given on relationships, romance and family difficulties.

Activity

Obtain a selection of magazines for teenage girls. Compare the problems and experiences of heroines in the stories with the problems of readers featured on the 'problem page'. What differences or similarities are there? To what extent are the stories divorced from the 'real world', in so far as it is represented on the 'problem page'?

Sharpe (1976), comparing the magazines of today with those of the 1940s, found that there was little change in content; the advice given by 'agony aunts' was, however, less moralizing in tone. Magazines for teenage and adult males follow the pattern of the earlier comics by focusing on specific interests and activities. They tend to provide factual, practical information, for example *Railway Modeller*, *Hi-fi*, *Shoot*, computer, and video magazines. There are also 'girlie' magazines like *Playboy* and *Men Only*, which offer photographs of nude women. Feminists argue that magazines like these encourage men to see women as sex objects without minds or feelings, and that they perpetuate notions of male superiority; many argue that such magazines demonstrate the way in which women are degraded in capitalist societies.

For older women there are magazines devoted almost entirely to fashion and beauty, such as *Vogue*, and also the weeklies and monthlies devoted to the supposed interests of housewives and mothers, of which *Good Housekeeping*, *Woman*, *Woman's Own* and *Woman's Weekly* are examples. *Woman* magazine currently sells just under two million copies every week. The articles provide advice and support for women in the roles of housewife and mother. The femininity encouraged stresses caring for others, the domestic role, the family, marriage, and appearance. Ferguson's analysis (1983) of women's magazines found a mixture of change and constancy in the content of these magazines since the 1950s.

31

Attitudes to some subjects had clearly changed over time, for example, in the 1950s and early 60s the subject of divorce was taboo, but in-depth articles appeared in the 1980s. Articles on health, horoscopes, travel, personalities, food, and beauty were, however, constant. In the three best selling weeklies since World War Two – *Woman*, *Woman's Own*, and *Woman's Weekly* – the theme of 'getting and keeping your man' dominated articles and stories throughout the 50s and 60s, with *Woman's Weekly* featuring the most clichéd stories. In recent years all three magazines had included articles on such issues as divorce, sex problems, and incest. New magazines in the 1960s, like *Cosmopolitan*, combined the theme of the 'independent woman' with the same man-searching of the older magazines. Ferguson argues that magazines like these help women to cope with their subordination and oppression. They provide an escape from the harsh realities of life – happy endings in the stories are the only place many women can expect to find them. She charts a decline in the sales of women's magazines since the early 1960s, which she explains in terms of competition from women's pages in national dailies, Sunday colour supplements, and television soap operas like 'Dallas' and 'Dynasty'. In 1958, *Woman* alone sold 3.4 million copies per week, while in 1982 *Woman*, *Woman's Weekly*, *Woman's Own*, and *Woman's Realm* together sold 5.3 million copies per week.

Women also read romantic fiction published by such companies as Mills and Boon. Romantic fiction is currently enjoying a boom while other publishing companies are experiencing a decline in sales. Most of the novels are written by women, for example Barbara Cartland and LaVyrle Spencer. They are written to a 'formula' that describes the romance between a hero and heroine, often in an exotic setting. Radway (1984) argues that these stories 'nurture' women who do the nurturing in the family. Romantic stories are a source of security for women who spend their adult lives creating security for others. Marxist feminists see romantic fiction as a product of capitalist societies, which like the rest of 'mass culture' conceals and disguises the truth of women's situation and encourages the view that the traditional gender role is 'natural' and inalterable. Greer (1975) writes: 'The domestic romance myth remains the centrepiece of feminine culture. Sexual religion is the opiate of the super-menial. Romance sanctions drudgery, physical incompetence, and prostitution.'

Television

Children's television contains the same gender stereotypes found in children's books and magazines. Although there have been changes, women and girls are not usually found in prominent positions. This suggests that television reinforces messages children get about gender roles from other sources, although research suggesting that television has a direct and uniform effect on viewers has now been discredited. There is a lack of evidence of the effects of television on pre-school children and a lack of knowledge about their viewing habits, although it is certain that their viewing is not restricted to 'children's television'.

Research in the last ten years has shown that males and females on television are highly stereotyped: males tend to be assertive, tough, and aggressive, while women are weak, dependent, and physically attractive. Durkin and Akhtar (1983) found that women played starring roles in only 14 per cent of mid-evening programmes – when present, they were mainly under the age of thirty and shown in a narrow range of roles: mother, housewife, nurse, secretary. They were rarely shown trying to combine marriage and career. Their research showed that children made sense of television sex-stereotypes using previous knowledge. In one experiment they found that young viewers altered their expectations when shown a programme featuring males and females in non-traditional roles; however, such influence is not necessarily lasting, and in a similar experiment with teenagers, the teenagers were less easily persuaded than the children. Television is also dominated

33

by male presenters, directors, producers, sound recordists, and camera operators. The only area where women are present in significant numbers is in children's television, and even here they are outnumbered by men.

Advertising

Advertising in a capitalist society is something to which both adults and children are exposed; it can be ignored to some extent, but never completely. In general the aim of advertising is to sell products in the most effective way, and in order to achieve this an enormous amount is spent by companies on market research into the likes, dislikes, needs, and problems of consumers. Advertising campaigns are intended to perpetuate the demand for particular products as well as to create that demand. Some advertisements use women's bodies – naked or otherwise – to attract buyers, but there is often no connection at all between the product and the female image. The partially-clothed women in advertisements for car tyres and alcoholic drinks are good examples. Feminists object to such advertisements because of the way in which they stereotype women as sex objects. Marxist feminists maintain that capitalist values encourage the notion that women can be assessed in terms of their physical characteristics alone – this 'objectification' of women degrades both women and men.

Adams and Lauriekitis (1976) claim that both sexes are shown in stereotyped ways by advertisements, and the effect of this is to reinforce the notion that males and females are fundamentally and naturally different. Advertisements contain five basic images of women: as the carefree girl, the career woman, the hostess, the wife and mother, and the model – images with which, according to market research, female consumers identify. The images show women as dependent on men, happy with men, and contented with family life. The message of consumer advertisements is that the product is the key to a world of harmony.

34

Tired or depressed women are occasionally shown in advertisements, but advertisements suggest that specific products – pain-relieving tablets for headaches, for example – rather than a reassessment of the female lifestyle, are the answers to such problems.

Advertisements for products designed to improve a woman's appearance, for example cosmetics, bath-oil, diet-food, encourage what Marxists call the 'objectification' of women. The message of these advertisements is clearly that a woman's natural appearance is inadequate, especially when it comes to attracting a man. Advertisements often encourage women to work on isolated parts of their bodies, as if improvement in one area will somehow magically alter the whole. Feminists argue that advertisements like these create anxiety and unhappiness in many women rather than acceptance of one's own appearance and shape. Advertisements suggest that there is an 'ideal woman', but this image is the creation of advertisers and exists merely to exploit women.

Language

Language is an institution that reflects social values, and is thus an important vehicle for transmitting ideas about masculinity and femininity, as feminists such as Spender (1980) have recently argued. Children learn that it is correct to refer to mixed-sex groups by male pronouns, and to use nouns like 'policeman' rather than the more neutral 'police officer'. The language people use reflects the way in which they experience the world and encourages them to interpret the world in specific ways. Feminists maintain that language, in a variety of ways, promotes the notion that males are superior and that females are inferior. Language also encourages specific kinds of femininity and masculinity. It reflects, for example, the view of femininity as involving a denial or suppression of sexuality. Adams and Lauriekitis (1976) claim that in our language, sexually-insulting words, for example slut, whore, bitch, are used far more in relation to women than to men. They list fifteen commonly used insults, all of which refer to prostitution, but are unable to quote one insult describing the man who pays for a prostitute's services. Insults to men usually implicate a woman rather than the man himself, for example 'son of a bitch' or a man who is 'henpecked'. Language, argue Adams and Lauriekitis, shows a basic disapproval of female sexuality, and reinforces the idea that 'nice girls aren't sexual'.

Adams and Lauriekitis maintain that the English language typically describes women as passive and men as active. Women are frequently compared to plants and food (examples are 'flower', 'petal', 'wallflower', 'honey', 'sweetie pie'). According to these writers, both men and women are compared to animals, but men are invariably compared to strong, aggressive animals like lions or tigers, while women are compared to domestic or baby animals like cows or chicks, suggesting their helplessness and need for protection. These ideas of masculinity and femininity reinforce patriarchy, or male domination. Spender (1980) argues that language in such societies is not neutral, but man-made: the deliberate creation of males.

Socialization also involves learning different speech behaviour for males and females. Children learn, for example, that swearing is acceptable in men but not in women; in women such language is considered 'unfeminine'. Men learn to control the exchange of ideas by interruption according to Zimmerman and West, quoted in Davidson and Gordon (1982), but they learn to interrupt women and not to interrupt other men. Farrell, quoted in Davidson and Gordon (1982), notes that the speech behaviour of women differs according to whether the group they are part of is a mixed or a single-sex group. In the latter, women typically speak freely and interrupt one another, but in the former they are typically silent and hardly ever interrupt male speakers. In mixed-sex classrooms, females are typically quiet, while males dominate (see pages 85–8).

36

Postscript

In the last five to ten years there have been a number of developments that suggest things *have* changed; that some people in our society are more conscious of sexism and are ready to change their behaviour to reflect this. Examples are manufacturers whose advertisements and toy catalogues are less gender-stereotyped; the writers and directors of some television programmes such as 'Grange Hill' and 'EastEnders'; television companies who have increased the number of women newsreaders and reporters. Although these changes must be acknowledged and welcomed, the evidence presented in this chapter (and book) indicates that there is little justification for the view that these are *fundamental* changes, or that we have now in some way achieved a more equal, non-sexist society.

Activity

Discuss as a group the reactions and responses of people towards those individuals who do not conform to traditional gender roles. Are the reactions to male and female non-conformity the same? How do adults treat children who do not conform to gender roles? Discuss the reasons for nonconformity to traditional gender roles.

Further Reading

Two highly readable autobiographical accounts of gender socialization are What Society Does to Girls *Nicholson (1977) and* Taking It Like a Woman *Oakley (1984). Adams and Lauriekitis (1976) Volume 3 is also useful, as is Sharpe (1976).*

3

Gender and roles in the family

Sociological background

Until the 1960s there was a strong suggestion from sociologists that the roles of men and women in the family in western societies were becoming increasingly similar. It was claimed that gender equality outside the home, shown by such things as changes in the legal status of women, the increased number of women who went out to work, improved opportunities for women in education, had led to an erosion of the 'traditional' family pattern of domination by the husband of his wife and of a strict division of labour by sex in the family. (Some tasks were thus seen as 'women's work', usually cooking, cleaning, looking after the children, and some tasks were seen as 'men's work', usually earning the money, doing repairs, decorating, with little or no sharing or swapping of these tasks.) The trend was for a change from segregated conjugal roles – a marriage pattern based on inequality between the partners and a division of labour as described above – to joint conjugal roles – a marriage pattern based on equality between the partners and sharing of family tasks and responsibilities, with no division between 'men's work' and 'women's work'.

Studies documented the increased employment of married women and the increased involvement of men in household tasks and childcare. In 1962 Fletcher wrote: 'In the modern marriage . . . both partners are of equal status and expect to have an equal share in taking decisions and in pursuing their sometimes mutual, sometimes separate, and diverse, tastes and interests.' Gorer (1970) wrote of the emergence of a new ideal of marriage – the 'symmetrical' marriage: 'In symmetrical marriage, the contrasts between the roles and characters of husband and wife are given little emphasis; what is emphasised is doing things together, going out together, helping one another, and above all, talking together.' The idea of the symmetrical marriage was developed by Wilmott and Young (1975). The cover of their book showed a father holding the baby with the mother looking on, while earlier in 1962 these sociologists had written

'the younger husband of today does not consider that the children belong exclusively to his wife's world, or that he can abandon them to her (and her mother) while he takes his comfort in the male atmosphere of the pub. He now shares responsibility for the number of children as well as for their welfare after they are born . . . many husbands acknowledge that, when their wives also go out to work, they have a responsibility to do more to help in the home.'

By the late 60s studies by feminist sociologists had begun to challenge assumptions about gender equality in the family with reference to two central areas – housework and childcare. These studies suggested that people's ideals may be very different from what happens in practice. It is on these studies that I wish to concentrate in this chapter.

Activity

How were the following housework tasks allocated in your family last week?

Task	Who did the task	Time taken	Was task shared?	No. of times done in week
Vacuum cleaning				
Dusting				
Food shopping				
Cooking a meal				
Making beds				
Washing dishes				
Ironing				
Mending clothes				
Cleaning a floor				
Cleaning windows				
Polishing				
Decorating				
Changing a fuse				
Tidying up				
Minor repairs e.g. unblocking sink				
Operating the washing machine				

When you have completed the chart, estimate how much time in total was spent on housework in that week.

Who was responsible for organizing the allocation of these tasks?

How would you explain the pattern identified?

Discuss the above questions with others in your group, and talk about your attitudes to these tasks – are they necessary/boring/enjoyable/tolerable etc.

Housework is a very good starting point for illustrating the differences in male and female gender roles in the family. The absence of the word 'househusband' in our vocabulary shows the extent to which housework is automatically viewed as a female activity. Men may claim to help with the washing up, cleaning, or shopping, but their use of the world 'help' to describe what they do shows that these tasks are not considered their prime responsibility, but someone else's — usually that of their female partner. If a man describes himself as a housewife, the Department of Health and Social Security will not accept this as a legitimate description, even if the man is at home full time doing housework, as an example from Oakley's study *Housewife* (1974) shows. However, many women, particularly those who are married, define themselves as housewives. Until recently, the DHSS required that a woman who wished to claim Invalidity Benefit had to prove that she was incapable of doing housework, while a man had only to show that he was unfit for paid employment.

The definition of housework that I wish to use is 'a set of activities that functions to serve a household and its members by providing them with a habitable place in which to live, food, and other necessary services.' (Compare with Oakley's 1974 definition.) All individuals and groups need these things, and recent studies have shown that in western industrial societies, they are carried out mainly by women. Just under 60 per cent of women were full-time housewives in Britain in 1977. Housework differs from most other occupations in several ways: it is unpaid, it is usually carried out in isolation from other adults, and it is an occupation defined entirely by the person doing it. There are no externally imposed 'rules', no boss imposing a time schedule or standards that must be met. According to many advertisements, housework is something that women enjoy and excel at. Men are rarely involved, and when they are, can only cope with simple tasks or demonstrate ineptitude.

Activity

Make a collection of magazine advertisements for household

41

and baby products. How frequently do men and women appear in these advertisements? Talk about the images of each sex shown in the examples, and suggest how any patterns you identify could be explained.

Studies of housewives

The subject of housework was largely ignored by sociologists until very recently. Oakley's study *Housewife* (1974) was the first to examine this area in depth. In her autobiography, Oakley describes how her own unhappy personal experience as a full-time mother and housewife led her to question the female gender role in the family – something she had previously taken for granted. Her study of London house-wives aimed to describe women's experiences of being housewives and to reach a conclusion about why it was that housework was an overwhelmingly female activity.

The most striking aspect of the women's experiences documented in this study is that while certain aspects of being a full-time housewife are valued – notably the independence and absence of a rigid timetable – and though some women were happy in the role, 70 per cent of the sample were dissatisfied with their occupation as housewife. This feeling cut across class boundaries. What Oakley's housewives disliked most were the never-ending character of the work, its monotony, the fragmentation of tasks (made worse when small children were present) and the lack of intellectual stimulation. The women who were dissatisfied were acutely conscious of their isolation from adult company and some talked of a feeling of captivity. (This theme also concerned Gavron (1966), and Hobson (1978) who found that desperately bored women at home talked to cats and counted passing cars in an attempt to relieve their feelings.)

Had these feelings been expected by the women before they became housewives? Studies show that few women consciously *choose* to become housewives; the presence of young children is usually the reason why women find themselves at home full-time, and take on the responsibility for housework. Many of both Oakley's and Gavron's respondents would have liked to continue with paid employment outside the home; the lack of satisfactory childcare was the main reason preventing this, coupled with the view that what made a 'good' mother was being at home with the children. Housework and motherhood (but not *parenthood*) thus seem to be inextricably linked. The socialization of girls and boys prepares them for this, as a separate chapter shows.

The average amount of time spent on housework by full-time housewives in Britain in 1971 was 77 hours – actually less than for some other western societies, as shown by the table below.

Table 2 *A comparison of data on housework hours*

Study	Date	Average Weekly Hours of Housework
1 Rural Studies		
United States	1929	62
United States	1929	64
United States	1956	61
France	1959	67
2 Urban Studies		
United States	1929	51
United States	1945	
Small city		78
Large city		81
France	1948	82
Britain	1950	70
Britain	1951	72
France	1958	67
Britain	1971	77

Source: Oakley (1974).

These figures do rather question the popular view that labour-saving devices introduced this century, such as the vacuum cleaner, washing machine and food mixer, have reduced the amount of time spent on housework. It seems clear that no such reduction has occurred, although there is little doubt that devices like these have significantly reduced the elements of hard physical labour and sheer drudgery. Housework appears to expand to fill the time available. Perhaps for many women, the amount they do serves to justify their position as an essential, if unpaid, member of the household.

Activity

Find out, by talking to some elderly people you know, how much housework has changed over the last few decades. What was it like without some of the equipment which is now taken for granted, for example washing machines, freezers, electric irons etc. You could also consult some household guides published in the 1920s and after (usually available in secondhand bookshops or libraries) and compare these with recent books like *Superwoman* by Shirley Conran.

Housework in contemporary non-industrial cultures

The ideas that housework is women's work, that married women should be at home doing it, and that it is low-status work are not found in the cultures of non-industrial societies, as anthropologists have shown. In some cultures housework tasks are done interchangeably by men and women. Cooking and food preparation are frequently shared, as is sewing and making clothes. This table shows how twenty-nine specific tasks are divided in the Tanulong and Fedilizan culture of the Philippines.

Table 3 *Tasks and their performers in Tanulong and Fedilizan*

Task	Performer
Domestic household chores	
Cooking	B
Washing dishes	B
Feeding animals	B
Skinning sweet potatoes	FM
Pounding rice	B
Keeping floors clean	FM
Gathering sweet potato leaves for pigs	FM
Waking up to cook in the morning	B
Splitting wood	MF
Cutting wood from the forest	MF
Preparing pig's food for cooking	B
Preparing cotton thread for weaving	FM
Weaving cloth	F
Washing clothes	FM
Sewing/mending clothes	FM
Washing dishes and pans	FM
Dressing and sacrificing chickens	B
Killing pigs	M
Distributing meat	MF
Cutting up meat for meals	MF
Fetching water	B
Babysitting	B
Keeping the child clean	FM
Feeding the child	B
Washing the child	FM
Cutting the child's hair	MF
Seeing the medium when child is sick	B
Taking care of sick child	FM
Counseling children	B

Note: B = tasks performed equally by females or males; F = tasks performed by females only; M = tasks performed by males only; FM = tasks performed usually by women; MF = tasks performed usually by men.
Source: Oakley (1981).

Twelve are shared equally, fifteen shared but less equally, and there are only two tasks carried out by one sex alone – cloth weaving and pig killing.

In non-industrial cultures it is rare for what I have defined as housework to be a full-time occupation. Even when it is strongly associated with one sex, that gender role usually involves some productive work outside the home as well. Kaberry (1952) describes the considerable involvement of women in farming arable land in African tribal societies – about two thirds of their time is spent doing this, the remainder on housework tasks. Studies of women's role in agriculture between 1940–1962 show that, in a sample of peoples from Senegal, Gambia, Nigeria, Uganda, and Kenya, between 60–80 per cent of the total agricultural work was done by women as part of their traditional gender role. Malinowski, describing the society of the Australian Aborigines, wrote:

'the woman's share in labour was of much more vital importance to the maintenance of the household than man's work . . . even the food supply, contributed by women, was far more important than the man's share . . . food collected by women was the staple food of the natives . . . economically [the family] is entirely dependent upon women's work.' (1963)

In these societies, women are expected to contribute not only domestic skills but others as well. In Yoruba society, a woman is not considered a suitable marriage partner unless she also has a trade. Girls are brought up to be independent – in Zaria, Northern Nigeria, married women are often the sole bread-winner in the family, but this is not considered shameful from the husband's point of view, as it probably would be by many in a society like ours. In western societies a woman's home-making skills play an important part in making her an attractive marriage partner; her career is viewed as unimportant, or may even be seen as a threat to her efficiency as a wife. Here, married women are usually expected to be dependent on, and supported by, their husbands (this is certainly the assumption of the tax and social security systems in Britain), although, of course, there are exceptions.

History of housework in Britain

In pre-industrial Britain the situation regarding housework was similar to that in contemporary non-industrial cultures. Domestic tasks were not the exclusive responsibility of women, whether married or otherwise. Guild records show that women were barbers, furriers, carpenters, saddlers, and joiners (although some trades were reserved for men). Also, as Hall (1982) has suggested, it meant something very different to be a housewife in the Middle Ages from what it means today. Housework enjoyed a high status at this time because it had the character of manufacture rather than service. Hall writes: 'Housewife in the fourteenth century tended to mean the co-ordinator and organiser of an establishment and centre of production.' The housewife was responsible for producing most of the essential items required by the household, including medicines, food, wine, clothes, and cosmetics; this entailed the knowledge of a number of skills. It was a contribution that was highly valued. Hall claims that it was easy for housewives to be involved in a wide range of activities at this time because families were units of production in the economy – groups that produced the things they needed, like food or clothing, for themselves on a small scale. The home and the workplace were one and the same.

The effect of the development of an industrial capitalist economy was physically to separate the home and the workplace and to change the role of the family from one of economic production to one of consumption of goods now produced on a mass scale in factories. As this development took place, the meaning of 'housework' gradually changed. Another consequence of industrialization was the growth of a middle class of people whose wealth was based on their role

47

as manufacturers. It was in this class that the notion of the married woman's role as full-time housewife first became popular. The non-working wife was viewed as a symbol of her husband's success in business. Her presence at home was also justified by increasingly popular ideas about maternal instinct (children were seen as more vulnerable and in need of protection than in previous times) and by the notion that a 'feminine' woman properly concerned herself with her family and did not go out to work. Oakley (1974) writes that by the last decades of the nineteenth century, the idea that 'work outside the home for married women was a misfortune and a disgrace' had become acceptable also to the working classes. She argues that to begin with, middle-class women did not actually *do* housework tasks as they were able to rely on servants, but by the time working-class women began to turn to the housewife role in large numbers, the difficulties of obtaining servants (caused by increased demand and alternative employment in factories for working-class girls) meant that there was an increasing similarity in the lives of middle and working-class married women. The unmarried working-class girl continued to work outside the home, increasingly in factories that manufactured domestic products; unmarried middle-class girls were not employed in significant numbers until much later.

It is fascinating to see how attitudes change, often completely, in a time of crisis. During the two world wars, every encouragement and assistance were given to women in Britain to abandon the housewife role for what were then seen as 'men's jobs': drivers, munitions workers, plumbers, electricians, welders, farm labourers, factory workers, indeed, to have 'stayed at home' at this time would have been seen as unpatriotic. In January 1945 there were 1,535 day nurseries for the under-fives to make it easier for mothers to take part in the war effort. When the wars ended, the nurseries closed and propaganda urged women to return to their 'rightful' place in the home, so that the men who had fought might reclaim 'their' jobs. This campaign was particularly successful after the First World War; by 1921 the proportion of women in paid employment was actually smaller than before the war.

In Britain in the 1980s married women are not generally expected to be full-time housewives unless they are mothers. I shall discuss this in the following section.

Childcare

Although the studies of the 1960s suggested greater partici-pation by men in this area of family life, recent work has shown that caring for children in western industrial societies is predominantly a female activity, and that most men and most women expect wives in families to take responsibility for the day-to-day care of children. The expectation that women will have a nurturing role of this kind, and men a more distant one, in relation to babies and young children is built into gender socialization from the beginning, as a separate chapter shows.

How is childcare divided in families and what is the exact role played by mother and father? Piachaud (1984) claims that childcare tasks take up an average of fifty hours a week in families with children under five. These tasks are over-whelmingly carried out by mothers, who are involved for seven-eighths of the total time. Two-thirds of the mothers did not have any spells of one hour or more a week when they were completely free of all childcare responsibilities, and nine out of ten found that looking after children was 'tiring' or 'very tiring'. Piachaud writes:

> 'There is an endless day for mothers. While some sociologists have written of the 'symmetrical family', the results of our survey show there is little symmetry . . . childcare remains low status work that receives little social recognition. It is an integral part of the perpetuation of sexual inequalities.'

When a couple have children it is usually the mother's life which changes most as a result. Despite the provisions of the 1975 Employment Protection Act for maternity leave, most first-time mothers leave paid employment to care for the baby, thus having a 'career break' – which is often interpreted by employers later on as evidence of a lack of commitment to the job. Only 11 per cent of mothers with children under five work in paid employment (Rimmer 1980) although it has recently been suggested that career breaks are becoming shorter (Social Trends 1984) and there has been an increase in the number of mothers with school-age children who work, although many are part time. There is only a very small number of fathers who have 'career breaks' to look after their children.

Activity

Find out what provisions are made for maternity leave and pay by the 1975 Employment Protection Act. What conditions does a woman have to fulfil, and are there any situations where the provisions do not apply? Interview, or write to, some employers in your area to find out what provisions they make. Are any of the schemes more generous than the minimum laid down by the legislation, and are there significant variations in what is offered? Try to contact both local authorities and private firms. Do any employers offer paternity leave; if not, why not?

Find out how many employees in each case returned to their jobs in the previous year, having taken maternity leave.

There is much social pressure on mothers in a society like Britain to devote themselves to their children, and this means that career or job takes second place. Working mothers are often considered selfish and above all, 'bad' mothers because they are seen as neglecting their children. Children whose mothers work may be described as 'abandoned' or 'farmed out', and it has been claimed that their future stability and personality are likely to be affected in a negative way by the absence of their mother. These views are not merely popular prejudice, but have been argued by child development experts and psychologists, notably Bowlby. The latter maintained that the constant presence of the mother was necessary to ensure the development of a stable adult and children who experienced 'maternal deprivation' might well become delinquent. There is a popular view that mothers, because of their instinctive love for their children, are the best people to care for them; this view is implicit in the writing of babycare expert Leach in *Baby and Child* (1979) as well as in the work of a sociologist like Talcott Parsons. Another aspect of this approach is that mothers cannot find true fulfilment as women unless they spend their time caring for the children they have borne – their biological children.

Activity

Consult some well known baby books (such as *Baby and Child* by Penelope Leach, *The Book of Child Care* by Hugh Jolly, or *Baby and Child Care* by Dr Benjamin Spock). What do the 'experts' say about the respective roles of mother and father in the process of bringing up the child? Are there any references to maternal or paternal instincts?

Cultural variations in the roles of parents

Is there, as many people believe, a 'maternal instinct'? Many recent writers have questioned the assumptions made about this by Parsons, Bowlby, and others. Badinter (1980) argues that the biological fact of motherhood can be interpreted in different ways by different cultures. In some societies 'motherhood' means a social role stressing close contact between mother and child, justified by the ideology of maternal instinct. In this situation pregnancy is a condition that restricts, as does motherhood, a woman's participation in other activities; indeed, a pregnant woman may be treated as though she is ill. In other cultures pregnancy and motherhood make little difference to a woman's usual lifestyle. Women continue to work up to the moment of birth and resume soon after. Turnbull describes childbirth among the Mbuti pygmies:

'The mother is likely to be off on the hunt or on the trail somewhere when the birth takes place: there is no lessening of activity for her during pregnancy . . . within two hours of birth, if the birth took place on the trail, the mother is apt to appear in the doorway of her hut with a bundle held in her arms. Within the same period of time, if the birth took place on the trail, she will continue her journey.' (1965)

The biological mother is not always the one who is expected to care for her child. She may be just one of a group of women who share caring and breastfeeding. Other relatives of both sexes may be involved, and in some societies the care of children is the prime responsibility of fathers, as among the Trobriand islanders and the Arapesh.

In Matabeleland, Southern Africa, the word 'mother' does not necessarily mean biological mother, as Moyo (1973) has shown. It is the oldest of the sisters in any one family group who adopts the title 'big mother' and with it the responsibility for bringing up not only her own children but also her younger sisters' and her daughters' children. This title is also applied to the senior wife in a polygamous marriage. Every woman who is a biological mother's sister, cousin's co-wife (in the case of polygamy), or a good neighbour is a 'little mother' and any one of these could become a 'big mother' if the current 'big mother' abdicates her responsibility for any reason. In yet other societies, children are looked after by paid employees rather than by their mother. In Israeli kibbutzim for example, it is still usual for children to be cared for from birth by trained nurses or 'metapelets' in communal nurseries; they see their parents for about four hours a day and return to the nursery to sleep. In some wealthier families in Britain today, including the Royal Family, it is not usual to find the biological mother in constant attendance; these families employ nannies to carry out the day-to-day care. In these situations little reference is made to a maternal instinct that binds mother and child, and there is little evidence that the children who grow up with these arrangements are disturbed or unstable or that their biological mothers are unhappy or unfulfilled.

The roles of mothers and fathers in western societies

Oakley writes: 'Putting childcare into the hands of women alone is not necessarily the best way of doing things or the most natural.' (1972) She argues that the notion of the existence of a maternal instinct arises in societies where some people or groups benefit directly from gender inequality. She and other feminists claim that neither mothers, fathers nor children truly benefit in a society where mothers alone are expected to care for children at home. Mothers suffer in such a society because they are unable to develop many of their abilities and express many aspects of their personalities. Although motherhood has a glamorous image, the experience of being at home with children for many women is one of loneliness and monotony, and, in an everyday sense, something that is far from enjoyable or fulfilling. According to Sharpe (1984) many mothers at home live in a situation which amounts to severe social deprivation.

Activity

Divide the class into two groups.

Group A: Interview some parents (mothers *and* fathers) who are also full-time workers. Try to discover whether they experience any clashes of interest between their roles as parent and worker: are they able to take time off with pay to care for children who are ill or to attend school functions;

does having children mean that they cannot devote as much time to their work as they would like; do they feel that they are able to spend sufficient time with their children; what are the attitudes of colleagues and friends towards them as parent/worker? Note the ages and numbers of children.

Group B: Interview or write to some employers in your area to find out what provisions they make for employees who are parents. Is time off with or without pay given to parents with children who are ill or when attendance at a school function is called for? Is there a workplace nursery or crèche and if so, how many places does it offer? Is it the employer's experience that parents are different as employees from childless employees, and if so, how? When you have collected the information, pool your findings in a discussion. On the basis of your findings, would you agree with the view that employers generally do not recognize or respond to the needs of parents?

The birth of a first baby can be more like a life crisis for the mother than the totally happy event it is meant to be, and it is something that can fill her with despondency and despair, for which the causes are not hormonal but social. Children themselves do not benefit from being brought up in a situation where they are likely to become very dependent on just one adult, especially if that person is not content. Many mothers suffer from post-natal illness and, when their children are older, depression. Research suggests that from a very early age children benefit from being able to make secure relationships with a small number of adults. If one adult in a family stops work to care for the children, the family's standard of living is very likely to suffer. Piachaud writes: 'For many families the result of the time costs of children is poverty . . . the time costs and foregone earnings are greatest with very young children. This means that poverty is most extensive in families who have them.' (1984)

54

When childcare is strictly divided, fathers in most families find themselves in a position where it is difficult for them to build close relationships with their children, and in later life, they may well regret this. Some fathers may wish to share with their partner in caring for their children, but in most western societies it is considered 'feminine' to like and enjoy looking after children, and men who do this may have to put up with mild ridicule, especially from other men who do not share their views. Earlier this century even pram-pushing, something that most fathers of today do at some time, would have been seen as highly inappropriate for a man. The demands of a full-time occupation, whatever the personal attitudes of the individual father on sharing childcare, make it extremely difficult for fathers to be as involved with the care of their children as someone who is at home. Since men usually earn more than women it seems less likely that the man will stop work. However, research shows that even when fathers are available, they tend to play with their children and take them out, rather than taking on less enjoyable but equally necessary tasks like nappy changing or feeding. It is usually the mother who gets up when the children wake in the night, prepares their food, organizes lifts to and from evening activities, and who clears up after them at the end of the day.

Many women defend their domination of childcare with reference to their husbands' incompetence. They may share the attitude of Chris:

'My children are part of me, part of my womanhood, mine, not his, and although I didn't mind him doing a certain amount, I didn't want them to go to him and not me for comfort. I always assume that I'm better at doing things, for example, bathing them. He had to learn things regarding childcare and it upset him if he couldn't do them properly.'   (Sharpe 1984)

People are better at skills they practise, but there is a strong suggestion here that Chris herself didn't have to learn how to care for the children: it came naturally to her. On the whole women do spend more time with children than men, and the unwillingness of some women to relinquish total control of one of the few areas they are thought to be expert at, means that men's efforts with children are almost inevitably going to appear clumsy. It has been suggested that, in denying men the opportunity to develop childcare skills, women are attempting – albeit unconsciously – to preserve a mystique about childcare that is not justified. This view sees childcare as depending more on common sense and patience than on any kind of 'expertise'. It has also been suggested that men, in order to avoid the less pleasant, messier, and more monotonous side of looking after children, deliberately carry out these tasks in a clumsy manner – sticking the pins into the baby during a nappy change, for instance – so that they will not be asked to do the task again. This is referred to as 'studied incompetence'.

Sociological interpretations

How have sociologists explained and interpreted the ways in which housework and childcare are allocated by sex in the family?

Functionalism

Functionalists such as Parsons justify a division of labour by sex in the family in terms of the female's greater biological suitability for a caring, mothering or 'expressive' role (Parsons) or in terms of 'sheer practicality' (Murdock) – by this implying that females lack the physical strength for many occupations. Functionalists have not written specifically about housework as this has been assumed to be part of the caring role. For these sociologists, a sexual division of labour in the family ensures contented individuals and an efficient and stable family institution: it suits both sexes and 'society' to have such a division. The sexual division of labour in the family is seen as 'natural' and inevitable.

Marxism

Marxists argue that a capitalist economy, and those who control it, benefit from the existence of a rigid division of labour by sex in the family. The fact that mothers/housewives are unpaid means that their labour costs the economy nothing. When women carry out a 'servicing' role in the family, men are free to concentrate on their work and to work more efficiently, thus increasing the profits for the employer. Housewives/mothers form part of a 'reserve army' of labour that Marxists claim is essential to the smooth functioning of a capitalist economy. This is a work-force that does not have regular, permanent employment but which can be used to supplement the permanent work-force in times of crisis (as in the two world wars) or when there is an economic boom. The presence of a reserve army also serves as a reminder to the permanent work-force that there is competition for work in capitalist economies; as a result, these workers are less likely to question the terms of their employment. Employers can thus exploit their employees more easily without facing a challenge. If a large section of the reserve army consists of housewives, the fact that they may not be employed can be more easily overlooked with the aid of notions about their 'natural' place in the family. Lastly, through careful management of the household income, combined with the self-denying characteristic of mothers/housewives, the latter indirectly function to reduce the amount of discontent among the male work-force by making the real effects of low pay and inflation less immediately obvious to the bread-winner.

Feminist perspectives

Oakley argues from a Marxist/feminist perspective that the mother/housewife role oppresses women and should be abolished. This would not be possible without a total restructuring of the economy and society, as the female gender role encompassing the housewife/mother role is essential to the smooth running of capitalist society. Women who claim to enjoy this role are not conscious of the *true* significance of this role in capitalist society (they might be described as 'falsely conscious'), nor do they realize their own potential as individuals. Such women have accepted the capitalist definition of what women should be; this acceptance is evidence of the ruling class's considerable powers of persuasion exercised through the socializing institutions of capitalist society, such as the family, the school, and the mass media. In Oakley's view, it is not the 'nature' of women that confines them to the mother/housewife role, but the demands of a capitalist economy. The potential and ability of women is deliberately suppressed by capitalist values, and the same could also be said of men, because capitalist values steer them towards a stereotyped gender role.

Some feminists disagree with Marxists on the question of who benefits from women in the family carrying out the mother/housewife role. They recognize that some men have more power than others, but maintain that it is men in all classes (rather than a capitalist ruling class) who gain from this arrangement, by being 'waited on' and relieved from the obligation of performing a set of unrewarding, monotonous tasks. It is thus in the interest of all men to preserve 'patriarchy' – a social arrangement whereby women are systematically oppressed by men in all areas. This would mean restricting opportunities outside the family for women, and maintaining a subordinate position for them within it.

Such radical feminists as Millett (1970) argue that both men and women are oppressed by any set of values that conditions them to play stereotyped male or female gender roles, be these patriarchal or capitalist values. Wages for housework and childcare, that some feminists have proposed as a way of raising the status of the woman's family role, are rejected by radical feminists who argue that such measures would merely confirm the view that this is 'women's work' and would do nothing to change the position of women in the family. In an ideal society individuals should be able to do whatever work attracts them the most and suits their abilities, regardless of sex. Writers like Mitchell (1971) argue that just as men and women are oppressed by gender roles, they are also oppressed by being conditioned to think that living as a family is socially desirable. She has advocated various experiments in communal living based on her conviction that there are many arrangements which will work well as all individuals are unique and have different needs.

Further reading

Two studies concentrating on the experiences of women as mothers/housewives in the family are Gavron (1966) and Oakley (1974). The experience of motherhood and its effects on women's lives is the subject of From Here to Maternity *Oakley (1981). A historical perspective on housework is offered in* Ordinary Lives *Adams (1982).*

4

Gender and education

How can differences in the choice of subjects by females and males at various levels be explained? How much has 'gender' figured as an issue in educational provision and policy? How do girls and boys actually experience 'education'? How are females and males distributed in the teaching profession and other roles within educational institutions? To what extent do education systems perpetuate or challenge gender inequality?

These are some of the many issues that have concerned sociologists working in the area of 'gender and education' which it is my intention to consider in this chapter. The chapter begins with a brief history of the provision of education for females and males in Britain and follows the above issues in relation to the different stages of education through which students in this country pass: pre-school and primary education, secondary education, further, higher, and adult education.

History of educational provision for females and males

The aim of 'equal educational opportunity for all' is, even as far as the official curriculum is concerned, a relatively recent one. Until the 1975 Sex Discrimination Act was passed it was legal for educational institutions to treat males and females quite differently, both in terms of the subjects made available to them and the quota systems restricting the numbers from a particular sex on courses. This treatment was justified by the belief that males and females had different intellectual capacities and interests. Some argued that males had greater potential than females, and that the treatment of students in schools should reflect this, while others maintained that although there was no relationship of superiority/inferiority, the fundamental interests of the sexes were different and required a 'separate but equal' treatment.

In practice, the class background of students had a crucial influence on the opportunities open to males and females. There was no opportunity for females from the aristocracy to learn the same subjects as males from this background. Girls were taught 'ladylike' subjects such as embroidery, music, and French, while boys learned Latin and algebra. However, there were some schools for females from this class (in 1868 there were twelve) and by the mid-nineteenth century, some colleges existed to train female teachers. For working-class girls, there was little chance of receiving an education at school or at home, and the subjects they were offered at school emphasized their future roles as wives and mothers – needlework, laundrywork, housecraft. In working-class schools girls and boys were often physically separated, even in the same classroom (by screens), and school outings were attended only by boys.

The idea of educating girls for their future roles as housewives and mothers strongly influenced the curricula offered to girls in all social classes. By 1882, cookery and domestic economy were subjects that earned grants for schools and were seen as a form of vocational training for girls; the numbers of girls taking these subjects rose dramatically. Boys were not given the chance to study domestic subjects, and were channelled instead into subjects like arithmetic. Although by 1895 some girls schools had started to teach maths and science and a few were in a position to coach girls for Oxbridge (although neither university awarded degrees to women until the twentieth century and Cambridge did not until the end of the Second World War), the majority of middle-class girls, and all working-class girls, continued to be offered a different curriculum from boys. This meant that although the barrier to women entering the professions was removed in 1919 by the Sex Disqualification (Removal) Act, few women were ever in a position to take up a profession.

Various official reports on education in the twentieth century stressed the desirability of a domestically-based curriculum for females. The 1926 Hadow Report, in addition to claiming that girls were capable of less prolonged mental effort than boys and prone to neurotic disturbances, argued that the nation's future prosperity depended on girls being trained to be good housewives. The 1963 Newsom Report said that 'the most important vocational concern' of girls was marriage, home-making, and childcare. It did not discuss any roles for males in family life. It stated that girls and boys have different attitudes to such subjects as science:

'A boy is usually excited by the prospect of a science lesson ... he experiences a sense of wonder and a sense of power. The growth of wheat, the birth of a lamb, the movement of clouds put him in awe of nature; the locomotive he sees as man's response; the switch and the throttle are his magic wands ... the girl may come to the science lesson with less eager curiosity than the boy but she too will need to feel at home with the machinery.'

This report was on children of average or below-average ability and it is clear that official reports had conceded that for some middle-class girls of exceptional ability, the curriculum might not be so closely confined to domestic issues.

However, provision for 'male' subjects like science continued to be poor even in many middle-class girls schools.

In Britain, the view that females and males have different interests and aptitudes, and that they should therefore study different subjects, has a long history. In the 60s, however, there was increasing concern about the way in which females were being disadvantaged by an education system that denied them access to subjects on the same basis as males. In 1967 a resolution was passed by the United Nations which stated that 'all appropriate measures shall be taken to ensure girls and women, married or unmarried, equal rights with men in education at all levels' and which called for equality of access to courses and subjects, and for both sexes to be offered the same choice of curricula, examinations, and qualified staff, whether the institution was co-educational or not. By this time (1964–65) the comprehensive reorganization of the British secondary school system had begun and most of the new comprehensives were co-educational. In 1975 the Sex Discrimination Act was passed: it applied among other things to education, and meant that institutions could no longer impose quotas for male and female students in any subject or course, or deny to one sex what was offered to the other. However, single-sex schools were exempted from the legislation, and as Byrne (1978) points out, the Act spoke of females as entitled to 'not less favourable' treatment, rather than the 'same' treatment.

Byrne argues that policy-makers continued to support the view that equality could be achieved by males and females being granted equal access to the same subjects or by their being offered different subjects 'of equivalent value'. The continuing differences in choice of subject and achievement patterns between the sexes have not been the focus of official reports on education or the subject of widespread public debate in recent years. Concern has centred rather on such issues as standards, sixteen-plus examinations, education cuts, and the curriculum, and in particular, the place that scientific and technical subjects should occupy in this. However, there was some recognition of the issue of gender in the TVEI (Technical and Vocational Education Initiative) scheme, announced in 1982, with the aim of stimulating technical and vocational education for 14–18-year-olds across the whole ability range within the education system. The scheme noted the concentration of girls in arts subjects, and the fact that many able girls left school 'unqualified to work in anything other than a restricted range of unskilled, low status and low-paid occupations'. It saw as one of its primary purposes the encouragement of girls to gain experience of technical and vocational subjects, and provided guidelines to schools on how this could be achieved. It is not yet possible to comment on the success or otherwise of this venture. In the CPVE scheme (Certificate of Pre-Vocational Education) introduced in 1985, there is a new compulsory common-core element for all students including such areas as personal development, social studies, numeracy, science and technology, information technology, and practical skills, many of which may have been previously regarded as the preserve of one sex only. This is a one-year course designed to replace traditional non-A level 17+ courses in schools and colleges and leads to a single nationally recognized qualification. The scheme also allows, however, for a choice of Vocational Studies, and it remains to be seen whether females dominate the 'Services to People' option and males the 'Technical Services' option, for example. Similarly, students taking part in YTS (Youth Training Scheme), sponsored by the Manpower Services Commission which is for 16–17-year-old school leavers, spend part of their time on work experience and the remainder on a college-based course. There is a compulsory induction course for all students, but college time is occupied mainly with optional courses and it remains to be seen whether female students will dominate in such options as 'community care' and male students in 'light engineering skills'.

Activity

Make contact with a school where the TVEI scheme is operating and discuss with the teacher in charge of the scheme whether or not it has fulfilled its intention of encouraging girls to be involved in technical and vocational subjects. Find out what measures were taken in the school to achieve this aim.

Nursery education

Children attend nursery school between the ages of three and five, often on a part-time basis. Local education authorities in Britain are not, however, obliged to provide this type of education for all children, and this fact, coupled with a shortage of private nursery school places, means that by no means all eligible children have access to nursery school experience. There are to date few studies of nursery schools and the part they play in constructing gender roles, but the work that has been done suggests that nursery classrooms mirror the basic patterns of later primary school, with girls and boys behaving differently and being treated differently from a very early age.

Many of the behavioural differences between boys and girls are very marked, according to Belotti. She writes: 'What first strikes one when one walks into a nursery school classroom is that the children are working or playing in groups of the same sex.' (1975) Boys are noisier and wilder, while girls tend to be placid and quiet. The two sexes choose different activities: boys prefer constructional activities, cars, movement, or games, while girls prefer sewing, cutting out, dressing up, and Wendy-house games. Belotti noticed that girls showed much interest in her presence in the classroom (as visiting observer) while boys remained involved with their games. Adelman, who used a camera mounted on a tripod for his observation of East Anglian nursery schools, found that boys readily expressed interest in this equipment while girls tended to hang back or cry.

Belotti argues that a pattern is set at nursery school which endures for very many years afterwards, whereby each sex comes to feel most at ease with their own sex group and increasingly mistrustful of the opposite sex. This pattern is imposed by the teachers in nursery schools and the 'hidden curriculum' (discussed later on pages 81–5) of these schools, rather than arising spontaneously. Research suggests that many nursery school teachers do think it correct to treat girls and boys differently, and observational studies certainly confirm that teachers respond differently to girls and boys in the classroom. Joffe's study of a San Francisco nursery school in 1970–71 found consistent differences in teacher behaviour, despite the fact that teachers tried to encourage children to participate in cross-sex activities – for example, boys learning cookery and girls woodwork. Girls' clothing and appearance was far more frequently complimented than that of boys, especially when the girls wore dresses, while boys were admired for fighting. Belotti found that girls and boys were constantly addressed as separate groups – for example, 'Look how well the girls have tidied up' or 'Boys! don't be so noisy!' – and that teachers often ridiculed in a gentle way the desire of a boy or a girl to take part in a cross-sex activity.

Gender is an important organizing principle in the nursery school classroom: although there is often an apparently free choice of activities, the sexes are often separate on the register, are sent to separate toilets, and are seated separately on more formal occasions. Delamont (1980) describes the toys, pictures, games, books, and equipment that surround the children as 'highly segregated and gender differentiated' implying that they stereotype the sexes and are designed to appeal to one sex or the other, but not to both. She argues that nursery schools do nothing to challenge any of the gender stereotypes the children already have. Belotti suggests that nursery schools are especially damaging to girls because they stifle creativity and independence, preparing them for a life

66

where they will serve the interests and the needs of males. Teachers indoctrinate girls on behalf of the males who control society, perpetuating behaviour patterns that benefit males and disadvantage females. She claims that such indoctrination may be unconscious on the part of teachers, but the males deliberately intend it to take place. Other sociologists have argued that the imposition of rigid gender roles disadvantages males as much as females. These arguments will be considered in greater detail later in the chapter.

Activity

Working in pairs, secure the co-operation of teacher(s) in a local nursery school for you to visit on several occasions (you will need to decide how many visits are necessary and practical before you start). Your task is to observe the class in order to discover whether a) girls and boys behave differently towards each other and the teacher and b) whether the teacher treats girls and boys differently.

You must decide in advance whether to inform the teacher of the reason for your observation, bearing in mind that knowledge of the purpose may alter her/his behaviour.

When your research is complete, produce a written report and pool results with others in your group in a discussion session. Some pairs in the group may like to observe primary or secondary school classrooms by way of a contrast.

In almost all countries the majority of nursery school teachers are female. In 1975 Britain did not have a single male nursery school teacher, for example, and in some countries the law demands that they should be female. Children are bound to interpret this as suggesting that women are particularly suited to looking after and teaching small children. Belotti claims that because nursery school teaching is of low status it often attracts less imaginative or independent women to its ranks, who are particularly unlikely to question 'traditional' gender roles or to introduce innovations into the classroom.

Primary education

'From primary days on, school plays an increasingly important part in sex role stereotyping . . . what you are taught in school, and what you cannot easily unlearn, is that males and females are different and unequal.' (Adams and Lauriekitis 1976)

An assumption made by many people about girls and boys in primary school is that because they are taught in a co-educational class in a less structured and timetabled day than secondary school students, they are taught always in the same way. Indeed, the Plowden Report in 1967 found little evidence of girls and boys taking separate subjects at primary level, except games. Recent research strongly challenges these images of primary schools and instead presents a picture of these schools as crucial in extending and reinforcing the gender differences children have already acquired by the age of five.

The few activities timetabled in the primary school day are, according to Byrne, mostly sex linked, and many schools separate girls and boys for crafts. She writes: 'It is commonplace to visit a school and find the boys playing football and the girls doing needlework, the boys building an engine or hutches for pets, and the girls cooking buns on a Baby Belling.' (1978) She observes that when primary school children work on 'interest-based' activities, their 'free' choice usually results in a sex-appropriate subject: here the 'hidden curriculum' (discussed in full later in this chapter) comes into play.

There is a growing body of research that suggests primary schools are staffed by teachers with remarkably stereotyped ideas about 'masculinity' and 'femininity' which inevitably influence their treatment of children, organization of classroom activities, and choice of learning materials for use in school. Observational studies have produced the finding that despite frequent claims by teachers that they treat girls and boys alike, it is girls who are praised for being neat, helpful, quiet, attractive, and clean but criticized for being rough, noisy, lazy, and untidy, whereas boys are praised for leadership, toughness, strength, initiative, originality, and adult behaviour but criticized for 'cissy' behaviour, weakness, and rudeness. This means that girls and boys who do not conform to the expectations teachers clearly have are likely to be seen in negative terms. These expectations force girls and boys into stereotyped roles; there is little chance for the boy who is quiet or for the girl who wishes to be lively and exuberant.

Some feminist writers believe that such teacher expectations are especially damaging to girls because the role into which they are steered is seen as secondary and inferior, and because teachers give girls much less direct attention in class than boys (a pattern also evident in secondary schools, as discussed later in the chapter). Clarricoates found that primary school teachers generally preferred to teach boys and saw them as more intelligent than girls, even when all the evidence was to the contrary: 'Boys are interested in everything and are prepared to take things seriously . . . girls tend to be more superficial and ask the 'right' questions simply because it is expected of them' [Primary school teacher] (Spender 1982). The qualities attributed to boys – independence, questioning, exuberance – were seen as evidence of 'free spirit', while girls were seen as neat and tidy, but not creative. Boys were ultimately more rewarding to teach, even if they were difficult to control at times. Davie, Butler and Goldstein (1972) suggest that one reason why primary school girls perform better than boys at reading is because this passive activity fits in well with the role that teachers favour for girls. HM Inspectorate found in 1975 that a (mainly female) staff made much effort to interest boys in mechanical toys, activities, and projects because these were rightly thought to hold their attention, but less effort was made to involve the girls in these activities and signs of interest in them from girls were often ignored. Byrne (1978) writes: 'The label "it's for boys" is stuck on far too many activities in girls' minds well before the age of five and is endorsed by far too many infant teachers in early school days.' Primary school girls have been found to be more anxious than boys for adult approval, whereas boys are more concerned about the approval of their peers.

Reading schemes

Many of the reading schemes used in primary schools, according to recent studies, contain gender stereotypes. In these, females are rarely found as central characters and when they appear at all, are often passive figures dependent on male characters. Women are frequently shown in domestic roles; in most books it is assumed that only males 'go out to work'. Lobban's study (1976) of six British reading schemes found hardly any working mothers in them and identified a rigid distinction between outdoor 'masculine' activities and 'indoor' feminine ones: the schemes showed 'a real world peopled by women and girls who were almost solely involved with domestic activity and whom the adventurous and innovative males might occasionally allow into their world [the rest of human activity and achievement] in a helpmate capacity.' Deem (1978) argues that girls and boys who have been socialized to think that such rigid divisions are 'right' will have their beliefs confirmed by such material; those without such expectations are likely to experience 'bewilderment'.

Activity

Carry out an analysis of some primary school reading books; you could look at the 'Ladybird' series and approach a local primary school for ideas. Look at the photographs or illustrations and read the text in order to identify assumptions made about the roles of males and females, perhaps counting the number of times each sex appears and listing the roles in which they are shown. Ask teachers who use these books for their opinions of them. If there are stereotypes, are the teachers aware of them? Are they critical? See page 155, *Appendix: Content Analysis*

Recent research, then, argues that children learn in primary school that different behaviour in males and females is 'normal', acceptable, and desirable. Critical attitudes to stereotyped gender roles are rarely found in the average primary school. Explanations as to why this is so are discussed fully in the next section on secondary education, and many of the findings in studies of primary schools also apply to the secondary sector.

Secondary education

Examination results and subject choice

Although there are different definitions of 'success' in education (for some, 'success' means doing as little work as possible or having a laugh in the classroom), many people see 'success' in terms of examination passes and grades. Statistics from examining boards in Britain provide some information about the relative achievements here of female and male students. At CSE and GCE O level, girls are more likely to be entered for examinations than boys, but a higher number of boys than girls leave school with no exam passes despite having taken examinations. For example, in June 1984 for Mode 1 CSE with the London Regional Board, there were 88,870 entries for girls and 80,507 for boys, while 10.1 per cent of boys were ungraded and 8.0 per cent of girls were ungraded. Since 1979 there have been rather more 16-year-old girls than boys taking the Associated Examining Board's GCE examinations: in June 1984 291,538 males and 334,750 females took O Level, with 15.7 per cent of the males and

14.8 per cent of the females being unclassified. Overall, a higher percentage of girls than boys obtain GCE O Level passes but this position is reversed at CSE. At both CSE/GCE O Level and GCE A Level, there continues to be a very striking concentration of male and female candidates in different subject areas, as the following tables show:

Table 4 *CSE Entries and Results in selected subjects*

		Number of candidates	Grade 1	Ungraded	Total
Biology	Boys	3,404	221	271	4,589
	Girls	7,131	484	398	7,362
	Total	10,535	705	669	10,951
Mathematics A	Boys	4,893	879	470	5,168
	Girls	4,411	606	535	4,596
	Total	9,304	1,485	1,005	9,764
Child development and the family	Boys	31	4	8	36
	Girls	3,965	350	422	4,236
	Total	3,996	354	430	4,272
Home economics	Boys	556	17	119	596
	Girls	4,197	326	411	4,428
	Total	4,753	343	530	5,024

Source: LREB June 1984.

Sociology is a good example of a subject that is dominated by female candidates. At GCE O Level in June 1984 there were 34,560 female and 12,039 male candidates from four examination boards (Associated Examining Board, Oxford, Cambridge, Wales). At GCE A Level in the same year there were 13,662 female and 5,113 male candidates from the same four boards plus the Joint Matriculation Board. (McNeill 1985) At GCE A Level, female candidates are less likely than males to attempt three or more subjects. This has obvious implications for entry to further or higher education courses,

Table 5 *School Examinations – Summer 1983*

| | Boys | | Girls | |
| | Thousands | | | |
	Entries	Awarded A–C	Entries	Awarded A–C
England				
GCE O Level				
English language	232	118	274	157
History	61	38	64	38
French	62	37	93	57
Maths (all)	220	136	177	95
Physics	135	81	51	31
Chemistry	87	56	61	36
Computer studies	31	18	13	7
GCE A level		Passes		Passes
English	19	14	45	33
Maths (all except computer)	78	45	27	19
Physics	44	31	11	8
Computer Science	5	4	1	1

Source: Equal Opportunities Commission leaflet 'The Fact About Women Is . . .' (1985).

especially at universities, where three passes are often an entry requirement. Byrne writes that this is important because 'graduate status is still the basis for a good deal of career-based further professional and managerial training leading to top jobs.' (1978)

Byrne points out that there are regional variations in the achievement patterns of the sexes: girls in South East England, for instance, consistently achieve above the national average while girls in the north underachieve, with the principal inequality gap occurring at A Level. Others have pointed to the association of examination success with high class status, but that within whichever class group is taken as an example, females are still likely to do less well than males.

Activity

Obtain copies of last summer's CSE and GCE (O and A Level) results from your school or college. Find out from these, for each level:
- the total number of passes and fails for females and males
- the average number of passes for females and males
- the subjects in which, in terms of entries and passes, males and females clearly dominate

What explanations are there for the patterns you have identified and for any discrepancies with the general pattern outlined in this chapter?

Sociological explanations for achievement patterns

There are few sociologists today who would support the view that the patterns described so far in this chapter can be explained in terms of males having greater intellectual capacities than females (although in the past, many male scientists tried to demonstrate the intellectual superiority of the male). Many sociologists see females as 'underachievers', implying that they fail to gain results which accurately reflect their true ability. There is considerable disagreement over the reasons for this, as well as over the reasons for the patterns of subject choice. Functionalist sociologists argue that factors 'outside' the education system, such as pre-school socialization and social class subcultures, are chiefly responsible. According to this perspective, the education system itself has a neutral role, and plays no part in creating the differences. Marxist sociologists, however, believe that education systems in capitalist societies play a crucial role in promoting values that support these societies; they see schools and other institutions as deliberately promoting gender differences, by actively encouraging males to be aggressive and competitive and females to be submissive and passive. Differential achievement and subject choice can only be explained, according to this perspective, with reference to the education system itself and the capitalist society of which it is a part. Emphasis on 'equal opportunities' in education, whether for the sexes or classes, is seen by Marxists as an attempt by 'the powerful' to deceive people into thinking that the system is fair, thereby securing their support for that system. As gender inequality is fundamental to capitalism, the inevitable purpose of education systems in such societies is to perpetuate gender inequality.

Interactionist sociologists have also paid attention to factors 'within' education systems in their explanations of differential achievement and subject choice, concentrating on observational studies in classrooms and describing students' perceptions of school and 'being educated'. Recently feminists have made a significant contribution to this area of the sociology of education. Some have worked in the Marxist/Interactionist tradition; others have rejected the notion of females as 'underachievers', arguing that in a male-dominated society, where males control 'knowledge' and the criteria for assessment, females will inevitably be labelled as 'failures' and their real achievements either suppressed or belittled. Some feminists have suggested that the only way for females to fulfil their true potential is in single-sex educational institutions.

Parental attitudes to female and male education

Functionalist studies on differential educational achievement by social class claim that class subcultures are based on fundamentally different attitudes towards the importance of education and qualifications. The middle class value education for its own sake; spending many years in the system beyond the minimum leaving age is considered desirable in order to achieve qualifications that it is assumed, will lead to 'good jobs', and parents generally encourage their children's efforts in school. The working class often consider it important for children to leave school at the earliest opportunity in order to earn a wage, the value of qualifications is doubted and parents do not demonstrate the same involvement with schools as middle-class parents. Sociologists like Douglas (1964) have used these ideas to explain why middle-class children gain better results and spend more years in the education system than working-class children.

Research on parental attitudes to female and male education, however, suggests that class subcultures are perhaps not as self-contained and separate as the above description implies. In all classes it seems that the education of males is more highly valued than that of females, and this has a profound effect on what happens to children at secondary school level – the point at which subject options are taken and the decision to leave or to stay on is made. Marriage and motherhood are envisaged as the eventual 'career' of girls in all social classes, and by the time they are teenagers, according to Sharpe (1976) and Spender (1982), girls themselves see their future in this way, whereas boys stress careers and work but rarely mention marriage or children. Many parents in Sharpe's study of girls at a London comprehensive (1976), especially those from an Asian or Greek Cypriot background, stated explicitly that education was 'not important' for girls. Boys were constantly urged to study, work, and 'do well', often in relation to a specific career whilst the common attitude to girls' education was a passive one. Sharpe believes that parents in general bring their daughters up to be protected and dependent: 'a girl is seldom given the opportunity to test, develop, and assess her abilities for herself, and is unconfident of doing things alone.' Competitiveness is associated with examination success and is seen as a 'masculine' quality. The role of parents in gender socialization is discussed more fully in a separate chapter.

Girls' fear of academic success

It has been suggested in some research that the female gender role into which girls are socialized results in their developing a 'fear' of academic success. There is a widespread belief in our culture that the academically successful woman is in some way not truly 'feminine' – implying by her success that she has priorities other than her appearance and her future role in the family. According to recent work, females in general are worried about the way in which males will judge them if they work hard and enjoy examination success, and that rather than risk male disapproval, they may deliberately conceal their real abilities. Komorovsky (1946, 1973), quoted in Delamont (1980), reported that US college students 'played dumb' and 'generally acted like passive idiots' in order to earn male approval, while Sharpe found that teenage girls deliberately neglected school work because they did not want to be seen as 'swots' or as 'clever'. The successful girl, comments Sharpe, is one who is less concerned with fulfilling the 'feminine stereotype', and Byrne also writes: 'Girls who do not perceive themselves in the classic media image may in fact have a hidden advantage.' (1978) Sharpe writes: 'Working class girls are more likely to feel the pressure towards the 'feminine' role earlier because they and their families are usually less oriented towards achieving high academic goals . . . middle class girls do not escape these pressures, but they may be postponed.' (1976)

A girl who is successful at school is likely not only to earn male disapproval, but also to be the object of open insult. Spender noticed in her classroom observations that boys frequently made insulting and often sexually abusive comments to such girls. Cowie and Lees (1983), in their research among fifteen-year-old girls in a London comprehensive, found that both boys and girls judged girls 'primarily in terms of their sex and sexual status' and that the importance of a girl's reputation was shown by a whole battery of insults, e.g., 'whore', 'slag', that are in use by both sexes in day-to-day life. According to

77

these researchers and to Spender (1982), academically successful girls are the object of explicit abuse of this kind. Cowie and Lees write: 'It is crucial to note that the insults might bear *no* relation at all to a girl's actual sexual behaviour. It is sometimes just "sour grapes"'. They observe 'even if the accusation was unjustified, few girls felt able simply to ignore the insult or to give as good as they got' (1983). This work claims that both mixed-sex schools and classrooms are characterized by behaviour that threatens and intimidates girls generally, and that this is particularly true for academically able girls. It is perhaps not surprising that in such an atmosphere girls demonstrate a 'fear of academic success'.

Sexism in the curriculum

The term 'curriculum' can be defined as 'all the learning that is organised by the school/institution, which may take place in lessons or outside the school'. To describe a curriculum as 'sexist' means that it concentrates on the interests of one sex and its supposed interests at the expense of the other. For example, history as it is taught in many schools, colleges, and universities, deals with the activities of males and with male individuals, literature is concerned mainly with works by male authors, music usually means studying the work of male composers. Deem writes:

> 'Where subjects or areas of learning do relate to women and their interests, they often do so in a very restricted manner. For example, domestic subjects are considered to be "feminine" subjects but are concerned mainly with teaching girls how to be efficient housewives and mothers – not with instructing them in aesthetic or general skills – whilst at the same time boys may be discouraged from taking such subjects as the skills involved are considered unnecessary to men.'
> (1978)

Subjects are thought of as 'masculine' or 'feminine', with the former widely considered as the 'hard' disciplines and the latter the 'easy' options.

Activity

Investigate the curriculum and syllabus of History and English Literature as taught at your school or college. Could these subjects be described as concentrating on 'male activities' and male writers? Where do the interests of females figure in these subjects? If there is a bias, how might this be justified?

Such feminists as Spender (1982) have drawn particular attention to what they see as the sexist nature of the curricula of educational institutions. They have pointed to the fact that these curricula are largely determined by males. Byrne (1978) states that 97 per cent of educational decision makers are male. Those who control curricula determine what is taught and who shall have access to various forms of knowledge. Such feminists as Rich (1977) argue that in a patriarchal or male-dominated society, all the social arrangements have been made by men to keep women dependent on men, and this applies just as much to the system of education as to legal, political, and employment systems. Spender claims that men present the curricula of educational institutions as 'objective', or worthwhile, factual knowledge, and have succeeded in persuading many to share this definition. She quotes Rich, who writes:

'objectivity is the name we give to male subjectivity, for most, if not all, of the knowledge that is readily available in our society has its origin in a male version of experience, and is therefore limited because it is based on nothing other than the subjectivity of men, who have been able to decree that what they do is right and what women do is wrong.'
(1977)

Spender argues that female interests, perspectives, and experiences are deliberately omitted from the curriculum and this means that females cannot draw on any tradition or stock of knowledge relating to themselves. In all branches of knowledge 'men have written women off so that they disappear.' Evidence about the many challenges and protests that women in the past have made about education is deliberately suppressed and can only be discovered by people willing to do much painstaking research, usually without funding.

Functionalist sociologists have not focused on the content of subjects taught in secondary schools and elsewhere as much as on the formal access the sexes have to these subjects. However, the mere offering of a particular subject to both sexes carries no guarantee that students will be taught in the same way by the same teacher. Sharpe (1976) argues that in subjects demanding manual dexterity, males tend to be given access to more complex tools and are able as a result to produce more advanced pieces of work than girls in the same class. This echoes findings for primary schools reported earlier. Teenagers are highly conscious of the same teacher treating males and females differently, as this comment shows:

'Although there are mixed classes for metalwork, cookery and woodwork, the work we do is different. In needlework, the girls have to make aprons and the boys make ties or cravats. When we asked the teacher the reason for this, she replied that girls are willing to stay in at breaks and finish their aprons while the boys like to go out and play football.'
(*Spare Rib* October 1978)

Sometimes the secondary school timetable may be constructed according to the assumptions teachers hold about what male and female students will or will not want to study. Byrne writes:

'By 1972 . . . the theory of "open access" was blocked (in

many of the two-thirds of secondary schools that were by then mixed) because subjects had all been labelled for "boys only" or "girls only" and cross-timetabled. It would therefore be impossible for pupils to opt for both areas of study.'   (1978)

Students have occasionally objected to this, for example: 'Our timetable was worked so that if you did art, you couldn't do technical drawing or woodwork or anything. I wanted to do art so I couldn't do technical drawing – I couldn't do both.'
                                                              (*Spare Rib* 1978)

Activity

Interview some students at your school or college to find out whether they were encouraged (explicitly or otherwise) to make a particular subject choice because of their sex and to find out whether they think such encouragement is justifiable. Interview some teachers to find out whether they think that male and female students should be encouraged to take specific courses because of their sex. Do males and females, students and teachers, have different opinions about this issue?

Sexism in the hidden curriculum

The term 'hidden curriculum' refers to values, attitudes, and behaviour that are not part of the official curriculum, but which are nevertheless communicated to pupils and students in educational institutions. Byrne writes:

'The hidden curriculum transmits to young people a collection of messages about the status and character of social groups. It works through school organisation, through attitudes and through omissions – what we do not teach, highlight or illuminate is often more influential as a factor for bias than what we do. Much of what girls [*and boys, of course*] learn and experience in the secondary years will condition their attitudes to husbands [*or other partners*], colleagues and workmates; their acceptance or questioning of governmental systems, their psychological mobility between the roles of economic provider, homemaker, worker, voter, citizen.'   (1978)

Feminists and Marxists have drawn attention to the many expectations about gender role behaviour that are communicated via the hidden curriculum. The hidden curriculum is a very powerful means of indoctrination because it is pervasive and subtle so that students and teachers may not even be fully conscious of its influence.

For example, the distribution of females and males within the staff of an educational institution may be read by students as a comment on the degree of talent, ambition, and suitability for various posts typically shown by the two sexes. There are more females in teaching than in many other professions (see pages 100–02), but they are generally found in low-status posts and concentrated in primary teaching. In 1974 although only 22 per cent of primary teachers were male, they carried 57 per cent of primary headships and 40 per cent of primary deputy headships. Byrne writes: 'The proportion of women in leadership roles (in teaching) has actually declined from 1965–74, and this despite an increase overall in women staff.' As already noted, there were no male nursery teachers in 1975, while the proportion of male teachers in comprehensive schools is steadily growing. Byrne claims that in colleges of further education, women's representation on the staff at all levels has steadily fallen. Two-thirds of principals and deputies are male, while in the universities, according to the DES in 1974, fewer than 10 per cent of professors were female, and only 6 per cent of all readers or senior lecturers were female, with only 10 per cent of all university teaching staff being female. Women dominate the teaching of arts subjects, men the teaching of sciences and mathematics.

Obtain a staff list from your teacher/head teacher/school
secretary and carry out an analysis of the staff in your school
or college. How many men/women occupy senior positions in
the organization (e.g. Head/Principal, Deputy Head, Head of
a large department or faculty, Senior Lecturer)? How many
men/women are at the opposite end of the scale?

How many men/women are cleaners, meal supervisors or
canteen staff, caretakers, technicians, secretaries, bursars,
counsellors? How many men/women are in the following
departments (you should adapt this to your own institution if
necessary): science, English, technology, sociology, mathematics, home economics?

You could carry out a similar analysis of staff in a different
institution from your own and compare and contrast the
findings, discussing the explanations for the patterns you
identify.

In primary schools children see a lot of females playing an
influential role, but they are still likely to associate men with
leadership. This message, and the notion that women are
usually in supportive roles, is increasingly stressed as they
move into the secondary sector. Certain areas will register
with the students as 'male' or 'female' fields. Throughout the
education system, students will experience a female domination
of non-teaching 'service' posts, for example secretaries or
dinner staff, that reinforces the association of females with
subordinate, 'backing-up' roles. Spender sees the few females
in leadership roles very much as 'token women' who are
present to give the impression that females have equal access
to such positions, but who are only appointed because they
have agreed to 'perpetuate male control of what is taught and
how it is taught'. Byrne found that men in leadership roles in
education had a stereotyped view of 'women's role in

teaching', viewing the female's role as 'subordinate, caring and more peripheral to central and major planning.' She also found that women teachers were less frequently groomed for seniority and responsibility by their [mainly male] heads. However, women teachers tended to see themselves differently from male teachers, describing themselves first in terms of their domestic, family role rather than in terms of their work. She quotes further recent research which has claimed that women teachers lack confidence, are more reluctant than men teachers to drop classroom teaching for administration (which a senior position usually demands), ready to defer career opportunities to husbands' careers as well as less persistent in applying for promotion. Byrne argues that there should be a policy of 'positive discrimination' in the appointment of women to senior posts in teaching because

> 'it is crucial that girls and boys actually *see* women in leadership, management, government, making decisions in their daily lives if we are to break the cycle of underachievement. As long as children see men taking the top posts and pay and women tacitly accepting this, they will believe what they see rather than what we say [about equality].'

Sex used as a basis for grouping and organization

In many secondary as well as primary schools, sex is used as a basis for grouping students for various activities. This heightens consciousness of sex and may promote the idea that the sexes have very different qualities, even that one set of qualities is superior to the other. The organization of students in an institution is yet another aspect of the hidden curriculum. Consider what children learn when they hear boys' names always being called first in the register, boys being called on to help move classroom furniture, girls being invited to help with refreshments at social functions. In some playgrounds and assemblies girls and boys are made to sit and line up separately; girls and boys have different cloakrooms and toilets. In most secondary schools the sexes are taught games separately for reasons described by Byrne as 'artificial', with negative consequences for both sexes. For boys, prowess in sport becomes elevated to an unnecessarily important level: it becomes vital for peer group acceptance and thus pressurizes all boys into sporting activities, creating much unhappiness and anxiety for those boys who actually dislike sport or team games. For girls, it 'endorses the exclusive masculinity of prestige sports which is an unnecessary and harmful message'. Byrne argues that girls' physical stamina and skill could develop similarly to that of boys if girls received the same encouragement: mixed games would also lead to students being grouped by skill for this subject rather than by sex.

Activity

Look at the class registers in your school or college. Do the names of male students always come first? If so, is there an 'official' reason? Discuss whether or not it makes any difference how the names are arranged.

Teachers' expectations of students

One reason why secondary school students (and those in the primary and further sectors) have different achievement patterns may be related to the different expectations teachers have of male and female students. Teachers may not be fully conscious of these different expectations themselves nor of the differences in the treatment of male and female students to which they lead. The suggestion of recent studies is that these expectations are communicated to students, who come to behave in accordance with them. The patterns already described for primary schools are evident in secondary schools and beyond. Males get more direct teacher attention in the secondary school classroom; they are helped more with the work and are asked more direct questions than girls. Studies of the way in which teachers mark their students' work show that when teachers assume they are marking boys' work, it is consistently given higher marks. One study found that in a particular secondary school, male teachers encouraged female students to behave in a flirtatious manner by behaving towards female students in such a way themselves. (Wolpe, 1977)

Spender (1982) argues that teachers of both sexes very often have difficulty in seeing their female students in any adult role other than a traditional feminine one. Stanworth (1981) found that male teachers could not envisage their female students in any kind of career once formal education was complete. Girls' future is seen in terms of marriage and motherhood and this is sometimes made explicit. Spender claims that girls are 'encouraged to choose subjects which – not coincidentally – help to make them economically dependent.' Teachers who attack or question the notion that women should have a traditional role are often very unpopular with their colleagues. Spender writes that her own experience of doing this led to her being 'accused of trying to turn the girls into man-haters and destroying family life, there were numerous comments about my own inadequacies and embittered state of mind [as a single woman with no children]' (1982).

Careers education

According to Byrne (1978), careers literature, films, and media materials are full of gender stereotypes, and this she describes as a 'growing problem'. Thomas and Steward found in 1975 that careers counsellors approved more of student career choices that conformed to stereotyped gender roles and that those whose choices deviated strongly were ranked as needing counselling in 'self-understanding'. Despite some innovatory material used in careers education, such as the *Gender Trap* series by Adams and Lauriekitis, careers education appears to guide students into traditional roles, thus continuing the work of educational institutions as a whole.

Students' perceptions of school and education

Male and female students prefer different types of classroom activity, according to recent work. Girls prefer to write notes or essays and are often reluctant to participate in discussion, whereas boys enjoy discussion and 'having a laugh' in class. Both boys and girls may experience secondary school as boring, but their responses in relation to this differ considerably. Although girls are often very ready to articulate their boredom to an interviewer who has gained their confidence, enabling such conclusions to be drawn as 'most looked forward to leaving . . . many girls object to the way that school treats them like children' (Sharpe 1976), they are much less likely than boys to translate their feelings into disruptive behaviour in the classroom, or to play truant from school. Stanworth (1981) found that in mixed-sex classes, the boys were able to manipulate the teacher by behaving disruptively when they failed to get attention. Spender (1982) states that 'in mixed-sex classes males are the authority figures; they do the talking and the lessons are designed to cater for male interests because, as most teachers acknowledge, if males do not get what they want, they are likely to make trouble'. At least one unpublished study has suggested that female teachers experience many more problems with disruptive incidents than male teachers, thereby implying that male students make particular attempts to manipulate female teachers (Brown 1980). Despite these findings, it seems that secondary teachers, like primary teachers, prefer to teach male students. Stanworth found that teachers treated boys much more as individuals than girls, and actually knew more about them.

By the time they are teenagers, girls have gained the firm

expectation that in their future lives they will be family-oriented, with 'work' as a secondary interest. Byrne (1978) writes that the fifteen-year-old girls she studied all chose traditional 'feminine' jobs with only a few unusual careers, and the lower the girl's ability, the more likely she was to be influenced by her family and to limit her choice to a local job. Even women who gain first degrees, she writes, have low career aspirations and see themselves primarily in a family role or in traditional work.

Activity

Interview some students at your own or a local secondary school to find out whether they prefer male or female teachers and why; ask them to identify the classroom activities they enjoy and dislike. Ask them whether they have ever played truant, and why. Do they think that one sex talks more than the other in class, or that one sex gets more involved than the other in disruptive incidents?

Pool your results in a discussion afterwards, and talk about how important the class and ethnic backgrounds of students are in shaping their response to school. On the basis of the information you collect, do you think it is true that boys and girls respond to school in very different ways?

As a follow-up, you could carry out observations of classes in your own institution, concentrating on the participation of males and females in the lesson, and looking at such things as the number of times each sex volunteers information, interrupts the other sex and the teacher.

Single-sex schools

In the state system of education in Britain today there is a pattern of increasing the number of co-educational, or mixed-sex schools; single-sex schools are now mainly found in the private sector. A famous study by Dale (1969) argued that single-sex schools encouraged stereotyping, limited female options, and were socially undesirable. Recent evidence suggests, however, that the academic performance of girls in single-sex schools, especially in such subjects as mathematics and science (which they are more likely to select as options than in a mixed school), is in fact better than the performance of girls in mixed schools. Boys, however, do significantly less well in single-sex schools than in mixed schools. It is findings like these which have prompted feminists like Spender (1982) to call for a reversal of current state policy in this area.

Spender argues that mixed schools are retained in a patriarchal society because of the advantages they give to male students. She writes 'the presence of girls is necessary in order to promote the positive image of boys. It is *against* the girls that the boys stand out.' The function of girls is therefore to act as a negative reference group. In mixed schools there is inevitably 'indoctrination and practice in the art of dominance and subordination', as the purpose of schools in a patriarchal society is to promote the idea that males are superior and females inferior. Spender claims that mixed-sex schools are in reality male schools which females have been permitted to enter. In single-sex schools, girls would not constantly have to defer to boys, they would not always be seen as less able than boys, and they would not be presented with males in positions of authority in the institution.

Changing the education of males and females in mixed schools

Spender acknowledges that her aim of single-sex schools for girls could not be accomplished either quickly or easily, and suggests a number of measures that could be put into practice in existing mixed schools that are designed to benefit girls. She argues that such subjects as mathematics and science should

89

be taught to girls and boys separately, this being a form of positive discrimination for girls, and she also calls for some changes in the curricula and teaching practices in secondary schools: 'I would like to see women teaching women about women – at least some of the time – and women assuming control and responsibility for women's education . . . but I will settle for a few sessions in a single-sex group where the subject for discussion is male dominance.' Byrne (1978) argues that changes should be made within the existing system of mixed schools, and although conscious of the 'underachievement' of girls, is anxious for changes that would benefit both sexes; unlike Spender, she believes that the present system disadvantages males as well as females. She states that in Britain there has never been any kind of national and public debate on the establishment of agreed minimum national objectives concerning the education for males and females, as a result of which both sexes are educated for separate roles which allow individuals little flexibility: females are educated for a home-based domestic role or for short term employment, while males are educated for a lifetime of continuous work but not for any involvement with the family they may have. Byrne (1978) argues that the subject option system, so much a part of the secondary education system, in practice leads to students making stereotyped choices in accordance with the above roles, and maintains that 'equality' cannot be achieved through such a system. She calls for the establishment of a common, or core, curriculum for both sexes which would ensure that no student dropped such subjects as maths, sciences, or domestic subjects, thus stressing the idea that the subjects are the proper concern of *all* students. At present, our education system 'turns out well adjusted, happy, generally knowledgeable sixteen-year-olds who have been allowed to spend all of their last two years almost exclusively on what they like and not on what they need, but this is like embroidering around the hem of a garment without checking that the material, cut and style are right'.

Further and higher education

On average, females receive fewer years of formal education than males. Girls are more likely than boys to leave school at sixteen, now the minimum leaving age; they are less likely than boys to apply for certain full-time courses in further or higher education or to be found on postgraduate courses at universities or polytechnics.

Table 6 *Going into further education*

| England | 1982–83 | |
	Males	Females
% of school leavers entering full-time further education in:		
Degree course	8.5	6.5
Teacher training	0.1	0.6
Other full-time education:		
HND/HNC/OND/ONC	0.6	0.3
Catering	0.7	1.8
Nursing	–	1.8
Secretarial	–	4.3
GCE A	3.2	3.6
GCE O	1.6	2.0
Other and not known	8.2	10.9
All	23.0	31.8

Source: Statistics of School Leavers, CSE and GCE, England, DES (1983) (Reproduced with the permission of the Controller of HMSO).

The table shows that in further education, males dominate high-status degree courses (according to Byrne (1978) they also dominate advanced courses at further education colleges, especially those in rural areas). The pattern of males and females concentrated in different subjects, described in the previous section, is equally apparent in further and higher education:

Table 7 *Full-time undergraduates at GB universities (UK domiciled students)*

| | 1983/84 | |
	Males	Females
Education	1,000	2,236
Medicine, dentistry and health	14,242	12,462
Engineering and technology	27,412	2,792
Agriculture, forestry and veterinary science	2,913	1,830
Biological and physical sciences	37,219	18,309
Admin, business and social studies	29,082	23,910
Architecture and other professional and vocational subjects	2,240	1,319
Language, literature and area studies	9,392	21,039
Arts other than languages	9,250	10,637
	132,750	94,534

Source: University Statistics 1982–83 Volume 1 Students and Staff.

Activity

Find out how many males and females there are in your sixth form or college, and if possible, how many applications by each sex were made for higher education courses at universities or polytechnics this year. Do your findings confirm the general pattern outlined in this chapter? How can the pattern you have identified be explained? Talk about your own reasons for 'staying on' beyond the age of sixteen – do males and females have different reasons for doing this?

Although there was some expansion in further education in the 1960s, Byrne (1978) claims that with the exception of non-vocational adult education classes, this growth has been heavily weighted in favour of male students, 'both in types of course and methods of study'. She believes that the 'male ethos' of further education colleges, which concentrate on technical and vocational education for industry and commerce, acts as a considerable deterrent to girls in the post-school sector. The grants system makes it difficult for many women to take courses at further education colleges, as married women are not eligible for grants. Explanations offered by colleges for the lack of female students on courses included: lack of previous grounding in science and mathematics; discriminatory attitudes from employers in relation to the release of women for study on the grounds that they were a 'temporary' work force; 'traditional' attitudes on the part of many girls combined with poor careers advice; and self-imposed domestic responsibilities.

Byrne writes: 'In terms of school leavers, day release for study remains one of the major and continuing inequalities [between males and females]'. She maintains that this situation cannot be explained simply as a result of student choice, as it is the courses that depend on employer sponsorship that are most heavily biased in favour of male students. Taking the example of sandwich courses, which depend on such sponsorship, there were only 13,000 females on such courses at polytechnics in England in 1983, compared with 35,000 males.

Activity

Approach your local college of further education for statistics on the number of male and female students taking college courses, including day and block-release schemes. Does the pattern for the college fit the picture given in this chapter? Does the college have a crèche or nursery to enable those with pre-school children to participate on courses? How do you think the participation of women in further and higher education could be increased?

Further Reading

Adams and Lauriekitis (1976) Volume 1 is a good introduction. There are many examples of studies which students could read here. Some of these are Spender (1982), Stanworth (1981) and Deem (1978).

5

Women, men, and work

The meaning of 'work'

It is important to consider the meaning of 'work' at the beginning of this chapter in order to underline the fact that paid employment is only *one* form of work. 'Work' produces goods and services; people work to satisfy material needs (such as the need for food), and other 'wants' (such as the desire for companionship). Marx argues that work is an activity through which people can express their talents and find self fulfilment. However, work is a social activity which can be organized in a variety of ways, and in capitalist societies, as Alexander (1976) writes, a distinction has been made between two kinds of work: production for use and production for exchange.

The former refers to work described by feminists as 'reproduction and maintenance of the labour force'. This is work done in the home, and consists of providing services for those who 'go out to work' as well as for dependent children and adults who cannot support themselves. It is not paid work, and is typically thought of in such societies as 'not real work'. It is work that women are expected to do (see chapter on 'Gender and roles in the family') and this expectation is the key to their position in the paid labour market, according to feminists. Also in the category of 'unpaid work' is voluntary work, again a type of work overwhelmingly carried out by women.

The second category – production for exchange – is that which takes place outside the home in return for a wage. The goods or services produced are sold to consumers. This work, according to Alexander (1976), is the work males are expected to do. The wages they earn finance the work done in the home, thus making those involved in production for use dependent on those involved in production for exchange. Some feminists have suggested that wages for housework would mean an end to the dependence of most women on men, but radical feminists reject this view (see pages 57–8 for a discussion of this idea).

Paid employment in Britain and other industrialized societies is characterized by a striking division of labour by gender, despite the fact that in these societies more women are spending more of their lives in paid work outside the home. In Britain in 1983 the female labour force numbered 10.4 million (some 40 per cent of the total labour force) yet in comparison to men, women workers are poorly paid as well as concentrated in a small number of occupations and in low-status positions. There are different views about the effect of work on women's lives (one is that paid work emancipates or liberates women, another that women workers are exploited at work just as they are in the family) and competing explanations for the persistence of the sexual division of labour in employment, and it is these areas I wish to examine in this chapter. Gender division in employment is a subject that has traditionally been ignored by industrial sociologists, who have either omitted women completely or seen women workers as a 'problem'. Classic studies of workers, such as Tunstall's *The Fisherman* or Dennis *et al.*'s *Coal is Our Life*, have focused, Delamont writes, on 'hard, dirty, highly paid masculine work of a particularly exciting kind' (1980). Many of the studies described in this chapter are the recent work of feminist sociologists and others who have wished to correct the picture of 'work' given by these classic studies.

Industrialization and women's employment

In pre-industrial Britain, every member of the family worked. Although there is some evidence of a division of labour by sex in this period, it is by no means the case that women were confined to a domestic role, even if they were married. (See pages 47–9). It was possible for this situation to exist because productive work was done in and around the home and no distinction was made between 'domestic work' and any other kind of work, as it is today. The separation of home from work, which occurred with the setting up of factory production, meant that it became increasingly difficult to combine domestic labour with wage earning labour. At this time, the notion of the woman's 'rightful' place being in the home was increasingly voiced by members of the newly emergent middle class. There was growing concern about the effects of women working outside the home (which many working-class women were doing, as domestic servants, and in the mills, for example), both on their families and on themselves. It was argued that economic independence for married women might undermine marriage and the institution of the family, that the children of working mothers would be neglected, and that certain types of work might impair the ability of women to bear healthy children. Hall (1982) writes that concern centred on women workers in factories and mines where they had a public presence and were part of a mixed labour force, rather than on women who were domestic workers and servants, even though the latter were appallingly exploited by employers. Underlying the apparent concern for women was a fear that male workers might suffer

97

if they faced competition from women as workers in these areas. Hall describes the changes in the cotton industry as it moved from cottage to factory production; this was an industry where women had made an important contribution as spinners, but were gradually excluded from this role as spinning became defined as a 'male' occupation. She explains the male 'takeover' in terms of men's superior organization and established position in the factories, rather than in terms of their greater physical strength or skills as spinners.

Alexander (1976) writes that industrialization led both to the exclusion of women workers from certain fields (as above) and to a sexual division of labour in the labour market which parallelled that in the family. In the early Victorian period in London women workers were not employed in skilled and heavy work, shipbuilding, building, transport, extractive industries (e.g. soap, manufacture, sugar refining), gas or on the docks. They were excluded from the professions, clerical work, the civil service, and scientific trades and had been excluded since the fourteenth century from the old guild crafts such as jewellery and carriage building. Around 1851, women workers were to be found in four main categories: domestic and household labour, childcare and training, the distribution and retail of food and other articles of regular consumption, and in specific areas of manufacture. She writes that male workers in highly paid sectors resisted the entry of women workers to those areas, often with the help of craft organizations or trade unions. The entry of women workers into a field previously dominated by men signalled a downgrading of the work. Alexander claims that the development of industrial capitalism emphasized the sexual division of labour that had been present in the pre-industrial family. Although women had had a productive role in this male-dominated (patriarchal) family, their primary 'natural' responsibility was always considered to be the care of children. With industrialization, males continued to be dominant in the family and also took steps to establish themselves as dominant in paid employment, by means of unions, legislation (see further on in this chapter), and by promoting ideas about a woman's 'rightful' place in society.

Married women workers

Women were not excluded from paid work altogether as a result of the above factors. Large numbers of working-class women did work outside the home, but in a narrow range of areas (for example, domestic service, garment making, and textile manufacture), many of which were related to the work women did within the family. Most of these women workers were single: in 1841 only 25 per cent of women cotton workers in Lancashire were married. One of the most striking changes in women's employment patterns in the twentieth century has been the increase in the number of married women working in paid employment outside the home. The table below shows the current figure:

Table 8 *Economic activity of women*

GB			
Women aged 16–59 by marital status – 1984			
% of women who:	*Work FT*	*Work PT*	*Are economically active*
Single	53	5	71
Widowed, divorced or separated	32	23	63
All non-married	47	11	68
Married	25	31	61
All women	32	25	63

Source: General Household Survey preliminary results for 1984, Monitor GHS 85/1 (Crown copyright).
NB: Economically Active includes the Unemployed available for work.

The increase in the number of married women workers in the labour force is a relatively recent one and began in the

1950s. In 1911 only one in ten married women was employed; in 1951 one in five, and by 1981 two in three. This increase was explained in terms of the need to raise the family's living standard. In subsequent studies, emphasis has shifted from explaining why married women 'go out' to work to explaining why they stay at home. It is now widely accepted that the married woman's wages are not 'pin money', but play an essential part in keeping many families out of poverty. Although some legal barriers to married women working have been removed in recent years, Oakley writes that 'the so-called revolution in married women's employment is perhaps more of a revolution in marriage than in employment' (1981). She points out that there has also been an increase in the number of married men who work in paid employment, as a result of the fact that more people in the population are married. Demand from employers has been a factor behind the increased employment of married women, but Oakley sees the increase as resulting largely from the desire of married women to escape their supposedly 'natural' role as housewife. This desire is the result of the married woman's changed situation regarding the bearing and rearing of children (due to the decline in the birth rate, the ability of couples to 'space' their children through contraception), and housework (carried out increasingly in isolation). For Oakley and other feminists, the irony is that, apart from a few exceptions, women have only succeeded in finding paid work which closely resembles that done by the mother/housewife. For Oakley, the key to gender equality at work is equality at home, and there is little evidence of the latter (see pages 40–56).

Employment patterns of women and men in contemporary industrial societies

According to Oakley, 'in all industrialised countries there is a marked differentiation by gender of most, if not all, occupations' (1972). Men are not only more likely than women to be in paid employment, but also 'command the majority of jobs carrying high prestige, high skill and high income'. The table below illustrates these points in relation to Britain:

Table 9 *Employment (occupations)*
Number of men and women employed in selected occupations, GB 1981

	Thousands	
	Males	Females
Professional Occupations		
Judges, Barristers Advocates and Solicitors	45	8
Administrators – National Government	40	10
Administrators – Local Government	22	11
Medical Practitioners	60	19
Economists, Statisticians, System Analysts, Programmers	78	19
Accountants, Valuers, Finance Specialists	204	23
Teachers in Higher Education	84	30
Marketing, Sales, Public Relations etc.	212	41
Scientists, Engineers, Technologists	896	87
Other teachers	239	408
Nurses and Nurse Administrators	48	539
Non-Professional Occupations		
Cleaners, Window Cleaners, Chimney and Road Sweepers	110	495
Domestic Staff and School Helpers	10	521
Shop Sales Staff and Assistants	130	701
Secretaries, Typists, Receptionists	17	861
Clerks	681	1,592
Total in Employment	13,765	9,151

Source: Census 1981: Economic Activity, Great Britain (Crown copyright).

In western societies, men are found in most occupations (except housework and childcare, as discussed on pages

40–56), but women workers are concentrated in a small number of occupations, most of these related to the 'domestic' gender role, and many of them unskilled. In 1962, two-fifths of working women were concentrated in five occupations in the USA, Sweden, Great Britain, Belgium, Denmark, France, Germany, Italy, the Netherlands, and Norway, and Oakley writes that this situation has remained stable in recent years. In socialist societies, there is some evidence that the sexual division of labour is less pronounced, but the same basic pattern applies.

Delamont (1980) refers to the concentration of British women workers in female 'ghettos'. In the semi-professions, they are found in teaching, nursing, and social work, while women manual workers are concentrated in service industries, food, textiles, and footwear production. However, the division of labour *between* occupations is parallelled by that *within* occupations, so that even when women are present, they rarely occupy high status or top management posts. Oakley illustrates this with reference to the Civil Service:

'there is [in the Civil Service] an almost direct correspondence between the status of a job and its gender . . . the higher the status of the position, the more 'masculine' it becomes . . . no permanent secretaries are women, whereas more than three-quarters of clerical assistants are.' (1981) [see *Table 12* on page 125]

Oakley also gives the example of the medical profession, showing how the overall number of women consultants is small, but pointing to their domination of such 'lower status' areas of medicine as paediatrics, radiology, and dermatology. She writes:

' "Women's work" is typically work that requires little training, little in the way of mental initiative and characteristically consists of short time-span tasks. It is also described as "caring" work – work that promotes the welfare of others, rather than the welfare or development of the worker herself.'

102

For Oakley, the parallels with the mother/housewife role are obvious.

Women's pay

Every commentator on the subject of women's employment has drawn attention to the fact that, in comparison with men's employment, it is very poorly paid. The sectors where women are concentrated – for example, in clerical work, textiles, or nursing – are some of the lowest paying industries. According to the 1985 New Earnings Survey, the average gross weekly income of full-time males over the age of eighteen was £190.40 and that of women was £125.50. These figures include income from overtime. In 1985 women's income expressed as a percentage of men's was 65.9 per cent. Cash earnings do not include such fringe benefits as company cars, membership of private health insurance schemes like BUPA, or expense accounts, all of which are more likely to be received by those in higher paid, higher status occupations.

Why are women's wages so much lower than men's? One reason for this is their concentration in low-paying sectors of employment and at the bottom end of the career structure within each occupation. Women also work for fewer hours per week than men, they do less overtime and fewer 'unsocial' shifts. One explanation for this is that their 'family responsibilities' prevent greater participation, but it is significant that this argument has not been used to justify the restriction of men's working hours despite the fact that they too have families. It appears that the Equal Pay Act of 1970, which came into full force in 1975, has made little difference to the disparity between male and female earnings, despite its intention to eliminate pay differentiation based on sex, and despite the immediate but temporary effect it had of narrowing the male earnings advantage. This Act initially applied only to men and women doing *like* [the same] work; given the sexual division of labour described, it was therefore unlikely to have far reaching effects simply because there was a limited basis for comparison. Snell (1979) argues that employers deliberately introduced segregations by sex in jobs where there had been none before in an attempt to avoid giving women workers equal pay, and claims that some employers deliberately hired male workers at very low rates so that their female employees would not be able to claim that they were being treated less well than the men. The Equal Pay legislation was amended in 1985 to refer to jobs of 'equal value', but it is too early to comment on the effect this has had.

Many people, including employers, have traditionally regarded women's wages as 'pin money', assuming that it is the male worker who supports the family and that the woman's wage is not really necessary for the family's survival. It is possible that lower rates of pay for women have been justified by employers in these terms. Land (1975) has shown, however, that there is little justification for such a view. She found that at least one household in six was dependent on a woman's earnings or benefits and that according to a DHSS analysis in 1970, the number of two-parent families with incomes below the official poverty line would have trebled were it not for the contribution made by the wife's earnings.

Delamont (1980) argues that the practices of male-dominated trade unions have helped to perpetuate low rates of pay for women. She states that unions have effectively denied women workers the opportunity to improve their pay by excluding them from entering many skilled, highly-paid occupations such as printing, boilermaking, and steel working.

Part-time working and homeworking

The table below shows clearly that women workers in Britain do an enormous amount of part-time work.

In other western industrialized societies like Germany, France, and the USA, there are also large numbers of female part-time workers, although not as many as in Britain. None of these countries has a significant number of male part-time workers. Oakley writes: 'Part-time work is intimately linked as both

Table 10 *Part-time working Spring 1984*

GB Millions Employees in employment	Males	Females	Total
Full time	11.1	5.0	16.1
Part time	0.5	4.0	4.4

The number of male part-time employees is assumed not to have changed substantially since September 1981.
Source: Employment Gazette, May 1985. (Reproduced with the permission of the Controller of HMSO.)

cause and effect to the exploitation of women' (1981). Part-time workers have little job security, promotion prospects, or fringe benefits. They are often very poorly paid. Equal Opportunities Commission statistics for April 1985 show that the average hourly earnings for all women doing part-time work were £2.59. A substantial number of these workers are well qualified women who work part time for family reasons, or who have been unable to secure full-time employment after a 'career break'.

Homework is a type of part-time work which has been neglected by many studies. This is paid work done usually on a part-time basis in the employee's own home, for example assembling Christmas crackers, hair rollers, typing envelopes. Men are rarely found in this type of work. Delamont writes: 'Rates of 10p and 15p an hour are common to homeworkers, who rarely realise how little they are being paid'. (1980) These part timers, then, are exploited even more than part-time workers generally, and have even less job security.

Activity

Find out how many part-time workers there are in your school/college. Record the occupations and sex of these workers. Interview a small number of these workers in order to find out what their reasons are for being part time, and whether they are satisfied with part-time work.

The majority of part-time women workers are parents. In 1982 55 per cent of women with dependent children (below the age of sixteen) were classed as 'economically active' [in paid employment] and of these 35 per cent were part time. Only 6 per cent of mothers with dependent children aged from 0 to 4 worked full time, but 19 per cent of this group were employed part time. The reasons why mothers do not 'choose' full-time employment are discussed on pages 50–1 and include difficulties in finding childcare, guilt, and spouse opposition.

Homeworking is an example of part-time employment 'chosen' by mothers because it apparently fits in more easily with caring for children than outside employment. Hope (1976) found that nearly all of the homeworkers she interviewed had dependent children. Homeworking was also the norm among the Greek Cypriot women in Constantinides' study in London (1977), but other reasons for 'choosing' this work here were husbands' opposition to their wives 'going out to work' and language difficulties. This example shows how working-class women from ethnic minority groups are often in an even worse situation than women in general.

Career patterns, unemployment patterns

It has already been mentioned that women's working lives are more likely to be discontinuous than the working lives of men so that women are much more likely than men to have periods of their lives away from paid employment. Women are often described as having a three-phase working life: from leaving school to the birth of the first child (in full-time work), while the children are young (doing no work or part-time work) and from when the children are older until retirement (in full-time work). Male workers expect to spend the period from leaving

106

school until retirement in full-time employment, receiving promotion and salary increases en route. Employers look on continuous service as an indication of the 'commitment' of the employee, and a 'career break' may therefore be interpreted as evidence of a worker's lack of commitment and may become a reason for not promoting or even employing that worker. Similar treatment may be given to those whom employers believe are likely to have such breaks in the future. Employers often assume that women, whether married or single, will eventually have children and leave work to care for them. They often ask questions relating to these matters when women are interviewed, whereas they rarely ask such questions of males. Hunt (1975) found that employers see women workers as less committed in other ways as well: women, it is thought, are more prone than men to take days off work for illness, they are unable to cope with responsibility and lack concentration. Hunt writes: 'the lesson to be learned is that the majority of people who are responsible for the engagement of employees start out with the belief that a woman is likely to be inferior as an employee when compared with a man' (1975).

Unemployment has been described as 'the most marked growth sector' for women in industrial societies' (Oakley 1981). In 1985 the male unemployment rate was 16.3 per cent as compared to the female unemployment rate of 9.8 per cent, and there were more males registered as unemployed than females (2,220,100 as opposed to 980,600), figures which at first suggest that this is one area where male workers fare less well than women. However, estimates put the actual number of unemployed women workers at twice the figure for males (270,000 as opposed to 130,000 according to the Equal Opportunities Commission). Many of these women are not registered as unemployed. One reason for this could be that married women are not able to claim social security benefit in their own right – this is the benefit that unemployed people receive after one year of unemployment benefit, or if they have not paid the required number of national insurance contributions. Women who are not in paid employment may also be likely to define themselves as housewives rather than as unemployed workers, whilst an unemployed male is unlikely to see himself in this way and therefore will register as unemployed.

Women part-time workers are more likely than full-time male employees to be made redundant. Because women's working lives are characteristically discontinuous they are more likely to be candidates for redundancy if the 'last in, first out' principle is applied by an employer. Many women in service industries, such as secretaries, typists, or check-out operators in supermarkets, are likely to lose their jobs in the future when these jobs disappear through the introduction of new technology. It thus seems reasonable to conclude that women workers are likely to be even more affected by unemployment in the future than they are at present.

Activity

Write to a number of local employers, for example a hospital, shop or factory, and ask for information on the numbers of males and females employed and the jobs they do. Find out how many part-time workers there are, what sort of turnover exists among employees, and about any redundancies or dismissals. Are there any sex differences in these areas?

Does the information you gather contradict the description of male and female work patterns given so far in this book? If so, how could you explain this?

Trade union involvement

Table 11 *Trade union membership by age*
            Employees aged 16 and over

| | Percentage of Trade Union Members | | |
| | Males | Females | |
Age	Working Full-time	Working Full-time	Working Part-time
16–19	21	24	5
20–24	47	45	21
25–34	56	52	29
35–44	59	56	33
45–64	67	58	38
65 and over	4	3	8
Total	57	50	33

Source: General Household Survey, 1983 (Crown copyright).

As the above table suggests, British trade unions are largely
male institutions. Although women's membership of unions
has increased in recent years, it remains the case that fewer
women than men become shop stewards or full-time union
officials. In other western industrial societies the picture is
very similar; in the USA, for example, one quarter of all
unions have no women members at all. One reason for this
situation could be that in recent years trade unions have done
little to promote issues of direct relevance to women workers.
For example, a recent attempt by Anna Coote at a TUC
conference to raise the issues of sex equality at work and
equal parental responsibility for children at home was greeted
with hostility by male trade unionists.

In the past, male trade unionists have shown overt hostility
to women workers. In 1808 hatmakers excluded women from
their trade, the potter's union tried to persuade women
workers in that industry to leave their jobs and return to their

'natural' place in the home, while in 1829 the Grand General Union of All Spinners excluded women and urged them to form a separate union. These examples show that male workers feared competition from women workers, who were often regarded by employers as more attractive because they were cheaper to employ, less disruptive and more docile than male workers. Women workers were often seen as undesirable unionists because they were believed to be apathetic and unlikely to support industrial action. In 1877 the TUC, then only three years old, declared that it was the duty of male workers to 'bring about a condition of things when their wives should be in their proper sphere at home instead of being dragged into competition of livelihood with the great strong men of the world'. Mackie and Pattullo (1977) comment that the welcome for women in the labour market was far from wholehearted and that in many ways the fears of male workers have never disappeared.

There are a number of examples, both past and present, of women trade unionists taking industrial action which can be used to counter the notion of women workers as apathetic and unsupportive of union action. These include the strike of match girls at Bryant and May's in 1889, the strike in support of equal pay by 1,000 women machinists at Ford's in 1968, and the strike by women night cleaners that was led by May Hobbs in 1971 (this union eventually became part of the TGWU). These show clearly that women workers have taken industrial action in order to gain a better deal for themselves. Women have often supported men who have taken such action, as the recent example of the miners' wives in 1984–85 shows.

It has been suggested that the explanation for women's lack of participation in the trade union movement generally is not due to their 'apathy', but to the way that trade union activity is organized. Most union meetings are held after working hours and away from the workplace – which means that many women workers who also run homes and 'service' husbands and children cannot easily attend. A survey by

NALGO (the local government officers' union) in 1975 found that 92 per cent of all branch meetings were held outside working hours and that few branches made any arrangements for childcare during meetings. In this union, although 40.7 per cent of the membership was female, only 17.2 per cent of union executives were female. There are few women general secretaries of any large unions in Britain, and although the TUC now has a women's officer and has recognized the need for greater participation and representation of women in the movement, no agreement exists about how this is to be achieved. The London Trades Council's Working Women's Charter, which was debated in 1975 by the TUC contained some suggestions that would have enabled more women to participate in unions as well as giving them better working conditions. However, the TUC voted against adopting these aims. The aims included a call for improved provision of local authority day nurseries, equal education and training for all occupations with compulsory day-release for all sixteen- to nineteen-year-olds, plus the aim to 'campaign among women to take an active part in the trade unions and in political life . . . and to campaign among men trade unionists that they may work to achieve this aim.'

Activity

Contact a local branch of a large trade union such as NALGO or USDAW (find the address in the telephone directory) and find out the numbers of male and female members and officials. When are branch meetings held? What steps has the union taken recently to promote equal opportunities for its members?

Work in non-industrial societies

The pattern of work in these societies is in many ways

similar to that in pre-industrial Britain, and provides a sharp contrast to the situation in industrialized societies that has just been described, certainly as far as a sexual division of labour is concerned. In non-industrial societies there are numerous examples of women doing what in Britain would be considered 'men's work', and vice versa. Women in these societies play a particularly important role in agriculture, often performing physically demanding tasks, and are economically independent of their spouses (see also pages 44–7). In some tribal societies women are involved in hunting, which is often thought of as a traditionally 'male' activity. Oakley writes: 'the traditional female role in wide areas of the world has involved women in economically productive work outside the home' (1972); in other words, the sexual division of labour is not nearly as rigid as it is in industrial societies.

The findings of researchers in relation to actual patterns of work in non-industrialized societies have been used to refute the ideas of functionalist sociologists like Murdock (1949) and Tiger and Fox (1972) who have argued that biological sex differences explain the sexual division of labour in all societies (see page 5). These sociologists claimed that the biology of males and females determines the skills they possess as well as their inclination for certain types of work, and that the cultures of various societies recognized these differences and emphasized them in the socialization process. Thus males were 'naturally' suited to heavy physical tasks, tasks involving decision making, and mechanical skills, while females were 'naturally' suited to caring for dependent people and to less strenuous work. Examples from anthropologists and others show that there is in fact considerable variation, suggesting that other factors besides biology are responsible. In addition, Murdock has been accused of bias: in particular, of only including those societies in his study in which the sexual division of labour confirmed his ideas concerning the influence of biology. Feminists argue that male bias on the part of functionalist sociologists has resulted in the perpetuation of the view that gender inequality is both natural and acceptable.

Employers and government's attitudes towards working women

The view that working women are a problem and that they are not behaving in accordance with their 'natural' role was, and is, frequently expressed in Britain. (See page 6 for recent remarks by Patrick Jenkin, ex-Conservative minister.) In her research into management's attitudes to women workers (1975), Hunt found a tremendous amount of prejudice against women workers: they were seen as less reliable and committed employees and were widely regarded as a wasted investment. In Victorian England, three themes were prominent in the objections raised to women's paid employment by [mainly] males: work would interfere with women's 'natural' reproductive function, it would lead to the collapse of family life, and it would place women and society in moral danger. These attitudes led to legislation ostensibly designed to 'protect' women from exploitation and moral/physical danger. Such legislation limited women's working hours or excluded them altogether from certain types of work, for example mining. Similar 'protective' legislation was passed in other countries like the USA. Protective legislation in Britain today is covered by the 1961 Factories Act, the 1920 Employment of Women, Young Persons and Children Act and the 1936 Hours of Employment Act. The main effect is to bar women from night work and 'excessive' overtime unless there is a special exemption order.

In the early stages of industrialization working conditions were by any standards deplorable. The Report on Mines in 1842 revealed the conditions in which women and girls worked in the pit: they were obliged to pull loads, sometimes weighing as much as $3/4$–3 cwt, along passages no more than 26 or 30 inches high. In these conditions physical fatigue and deformities were common results, and women reportedly had more difficult births and less healthy babies if they had been employed in the mines. The need for protective legislation was clear, but feminists point out that male workers who had to endure the same conditions were never the object of such legislation. This fact suggests, they claim, that the real intention of such legislation was exclusion for women rather than protection. One result of the legislation was to reduce the earning capacity of women workers, thereby increasing their dependence on the male wage earner. According to some feminists, this was the perpetuation of patriarchy (male dominance) both in the workplace and in the home. They point out that the legislation was passed by a largely male parliament.

In Britain today some feminists argue that all protective legislation should be abolished in the name of equality. Others maintain that abolition would not bring about a material improvement in women's lives and that instead the legislation should be extended to male workers as well. The view of the Equal Opportunities Commission is that such laws are discriminatory and inhibit women's opportunities. A 1979 EOC survey found that 60 per cent of women were in favour of repealing shift work and overtime restrictions and that 40 per cent wanted all obstacles to women doing night work removed.

Other legislation in Britain concerned with women's work includes the Equal Pay Act (discussed on page 103) and the Sex Discrimination Act of 1975. The latter made it illegal to discriminate against a person on the grounds of their sex, for example by refusing them a job, training, or promotion. However, there are some areas where this legislation does not apply: employment in single-sex institutions, where customers' preferences make it essential to employ a woman (or a man), where communal living arrangements are part of the job, and where it would be offensive to 'public taste or decency' for a woman (or a man) to do the job. The Employment Protection Act (1975) also gave women the right to paid maternity leave and the right of return to their post after the birth of a child.

However, this was only the case for women who had been in continuous employment with the same employer for two years prior to the birth; the legislation did not apply to small firms, nor were these rights guaranteed for part-time workers.

The role of the Equal Opportunities Commission in Britain is to monitor the operation of these laws and to support individuals who bring cases of unfair treatment before the courts. The EOC also publishes statistics showing the relative involvement of men and women in work and other areas. Feminists have little faith in such organizations as the EOC and the legislation described above. Coussins (1980) argues that the long list of areas where the legislation does not apply is an indication of the government's lack of commitment to genuine sex equality. Her description of the Sex Discrimination Act is 'feeble'.

Women's attitudes to paid work

Engels and Marx predicted that paid work would liberate women by freeing them from economic dependence on their husbands and from the housewife role in the family. Rowbotham (1973) has argued more recently that women who work outside the home must eventually confront the contradiction between the demands of this role and the demands of the housewife/family role, and that the result will be increased demands from women, increased criticism of their 'traditional' role. In the light of these ideas, it is relevant to ask how women themselves feel about the paid work they do.

Martin and Roberts found that 'most married women of working age still felt that [paid] work was less central to their lives and that a home and children were a woman's real aim and her main job' (1980). Pollert found among women factory workers a 'stoical endurance towards shouldering the double burden of home and work mixed with a sense of injustice' (1981). The women she studied were caught in a 'perpetual conflict of time, priorities and ideas'. Studies like these suggest that women in general tend to accept a subordinate position at work rather than rebelling against it. It would also be difficult to argue that women are economically independent in the sense that Marx meant, in view of the situation with regard to pay and opportunities, or that in any sense work has freed them from responsibility for domestic chores (see chapter 3). Recently, however, Sharpe (1984) showed that working had a central place in the lives of her sample of working mothers, and that it was a vital part of their self image, and Martin and Roberts suggested that younger women were increasingly likely to give work a high priority. For the majority of girls leaving school, however, marriage is still the most important aim, whereas for boys, it is having a job. This has been shown recently in the work of both Sharpe and Wilson (1978). Wilson writes that the 13–15-year-old girls in her study were

> 'faced with limited educational opportunities and the prospect of dead end jobs . . . they had a high commitment to marriage at an early age . . . marriage provided the easiest and most obvious means of escape from the parental home and also signified the transition into adulthood for the girls.'

The two areas Wilson drew her samples from were traditional working-class areas in a northern city. Marriage rather than a career remains an aim for middle-class girls as well, though they are likely to opt for marriage at a later age.

Dual labour market theory

This is an idea which has been used to explain the sexual division of labour in paid employment. Barron and Norris (1978) claim that in capitalist societies two distinct markets for labour develop: the primary sector (characterized by secure, well-paid work with good promotion prospects in a safe and pleasant environment), and the secondary sector (characterized by insecure, poorly-paid often unskilled jobs).

116

Employers allocate individual workers to the sector considered most suitable for their perceived talents, qualifications, and skills. Because of the stereotyped beliefs employers frequently hold about the qualities of women workers, women are much more likely than men to be allocated jobs in the secondary sector. The academic qualifications women increasingly hold make little difference to this pattern. Male workers too are viewed in stereotyped ways: they are expected to fit into a career structure at work, give continuous service, and be devoted to the interests of the firm. Employers control entry to primary sector jobs 'behind the scenes': they often take on inexperienced workers of both sexes to begin with, and the allocation to the primary sector takes place later as employees are selected for training and promotion.

Reserve army of labour

Derived from Marxist traditions, this theory sees women workers as a crucial constituent of the 'reserve army of labour' which develops in all capitalist societies. The existence of such a group of workers aids the smooth running of a capitalist economy and the interests of those who control it (see page 57). The values promoted in such a society lead to women being viewed as 'disposable workers' and to the family role being seen as their primary role – a role to which paid work must take second place.

Recently some Marxist feminists have questioned the notion that female workers are particularly 'disposable' in times of economic crisis. Bruegel (1982) examined this view of women in the light of the experiences of women workers in Britain in the period 1974–78 and concluded that, generally speaking, the continued expansion of service industries in this period had the effect of protecting women's employment opportunities from the worst effects of the crisis. As individuals, however, women in this period were more likely to face redundancy when compared to men in similar circumstances. Women workers, especially part timers, suffered

117

from greater job loss than male workers, and Bruegel points out that the 'protection' of their jobs was based almost entirely on the 'cheapness of female labour'. She argues that the low pay offered to women in service jobs virtually ruled out any wholesale takeover by men, even though unemployment was high.

Bruegel and others argue that the position of women in the service sector is likely to deteriorate severely in the near future as new forms of technology, such as microprocessors, are adopted by employers in preference to the women workers who currently do such jobs as record keeping, clerical work, or check-out operating. This has already begun to happen in countries like Germany and the USA. She writes: 'Many groups of women who have traditionally regarded their jobs as secure will find themselves threatened with rationalization on a scale comparable to the wholesale elimination of jobs in the traditional male strongholds – mining, railways and docks'. Bruegel accepts the reserve army of labour model, but with qualifications.

Further Reading

An introduction here is Adams and Lauriekitis (1976) Volume 1, also Mackie and Pattullo (1977). More ambitious readers may try the section on 'Employment and Training' in Whitelegg et al. (1982) or Pollert (1981).

6

Women, men, and politics

'Politics' defined

The Collins English Dictionary defines politics as 'the practice or study of the art or science of forming, directing and administering states and other political units: the art and science of government'. Such a traditional definition of politics is shared by many political scientists and may be found in standard textbooks on government. The reader also learns from the dictionary that 'politics' refers to the 'complex or aggregate of relationships of *men* (my emphasis) in society, especially those involving authority or power'. The first part of this chapter will consider why it is the case that women remain largely uninvolved in the formal politics of government in many societies, despite their having in some cases fought long and hard to acquire the rights and duties of citizens in those societies.

However, 'politics' also has a wider definition than this, as suggested by the following quotation from a US women's group in 1969:

'Our politics begin with our feelings . . . the political unit in which we can discover, share and explore our feelings is the small group. Raising our collective consciousness is not a process that begins and ends, but is continuous and necessary given the enormous pressure placed on us everywhere to deny our own perceptions.'

(San Francisco Redstockings, 1969)

According to the above, the personal is political: people's private lives and experiences, particularly if they are oppressed, are more significant and more important to study than questions of voting patterns or styles of government. Thus, the second part of the chapter will look at the campaigns and history of feminists who share this wider definition of 'politics', and at some of the issues raised by the feminist movement, for example the question of how political awareness or consciousness might be spread.

Women in the British Parliament

Parliament in Britain is by any standards a male-dominated institution. In Britain women won the vote on equal terms with men in 1928, but despite this they have never managed to hold as many as 5 per cent of the seats in the House of Commons nor have they ever constituted a significant proportion of the total membership of the House of Lords. In 1986 there were 27 women MPs out of a total of 650 and 46 women life peers out of a total of 355 life peers. Between and after the two world wars the number of women MPs increased slowly, and between 1955–74 their numbers fluctuated between 23 and 29, but in 1979, the year of the election of Margaret Thatcher as the first British woman Prime Minister, there were only 19 woman MPs. Today there are no women in Mrs Thatcher's cabinet other than herself.

From 1929 to the present day there has been an increase in the number of female candidates standing in parliamentary elections in Britain, but women candidates still only form 8 per cent of the total number of candidates. In the last election, as in previous years, the Labour party fielded more female candidates than the Conservatives, and the increase in female candidates reflects a general increase in the number of candidates fielded by smaller political parties, according to Hills (1978). This study shows that women candidates are usually chosen to fight marginal seats which they have little chance of winning. Stacey and Price (1981) comment that as chances of electoral success increase, so does competition from men: this is shown by the decline in the number of women candidates for the Scottish National Party following its electoral successes in the 70s. Once elected, a woman's chances of gaining a senior position in government are small. Although there are women in all parties, there are few women in the top levels of either the constituency or national party organizations. Women MPs tend to gain appointments in what many would see as the 'traditional' female areas of health, education, or consumer affairs (take for example Edwina Currie, the Junior Health Minister).

Mellors (1978), comparing women and men MPs, found that women MPs are more likely than men to be over forty, married, middle-class, university educated, and with grown-up children. Currell (1974) found that women MPs often came from 'political' families or from families with a strong tradition of public service, while Oakley (1981) states that women MPs have three basic characteristics: first, they are *not* feminists, second, many enter politics in the footsteps of a man, and third, their political views are not, on the whole, left wing.

Activity

Find out whether or not the following female politicians possess the three characteristics mentioned by Oakley: Margaret Thatcher, Corazon Aquino, Indira Gandhi, Eva Peron, Shirley Williams, Harriet Harman.

Do they also fit Mellors' picture of the 'typical' female politician? You can collect information about these politicians from newspapers, or books and periodicals in the library.

Oakley observes that opposers of female suffrage in Britain would have been 'pleasantly surprised' to discover that women MPs have these characteristics because they apparently feared that if women ever participated in politics, they would attack and overturn the established order of things.

According to Barbara Castle, who held office in the Wilson government and later became an MEP in the European Parliament, women MPs experience Westminster as a somewhat hostile, anti-female environment (Stacey and Price 1981). As a Minister, she found that there were no women's lavatories or changing rooms available for her, and that the House of Commons was rather like a male club, in which a woman was excluded from much of the informal colleagueship. Women MPs face constant criticism no matter what they do, according to Delamont (1980). Their clothes, hair, speech, lifestyle, and behaviour are all subject to unremitting appraisal. If married, they may be accused of neglecting their family; if single, they are out of touch with family life. They may be accused of ignoring women's interests if they do not pursue feminist policies, but if they do, they are held to be trivializing politics and neglecting 'real' issues. Delamont comments: 'In short, the woman in the political élite suffers all the disadvantages of any professional woman, with none of the compensations of power and authority which might soften the hardship.'

Activity

Collect articles which refer to male and female MPs from national newspapers. Is there any difference in the remarks made about them in relation to the factors mentioned by Delamont (above)? You may be able to consult back copies of newspapers in the library in order to compare and contrast statements made about the following British MPs as a follow-up: Cecil Parkinson, Shirley Williams, Margaret Thatcher, Michael Foot, Helene Hayman.

Women in politics outside Britain

Newland's study in 1975 of the proportion of seats held by women in thirty-five national legislative bodies showed that, as in Britain, women play little part in such organizations. They rarely account for as much as 10 per cent of the total membership of these bodies. The proportion of women in national legislatures ranged from none in Panama, to 7 per cent in the West German Bundestag and 3 per cent in the US Congress. The main exceptions were Scandinavian countries and some one-party states like the USSR, China, and Guinea, but as Newland points out, in many one-party states the centre of real power is found less in the legislature than in the party itself. In such countries women are largely absent from party hierarchies. Those who take part are 'cannon fodder; they knock on doors, answer telephones, hand out leaflets.'

Stacey and Price (1981) write that the underrepresentation of women is especially marked in international organizations, whatever their size, purpose, powers, or structure. There seems to be a considerable discrepancy between the stance adopted by the United Nations on the position of women in society and the numbers of women who work within the UN: as Thom (1980) pointed out, in 1974 women formed only 3 per cent of the delegates to the UN General Assembly and 10.3 per cent of the staff in Permanent Missions. The one exception to this picture is the European Assembly, where women formed 16 per cent of MEPs in 1979. Stacey and Price claim that this figure is higher than usual because the European Assembly is widely recognized as being less prestigious or influential than other bodies, as reflected by the low turn-out of voters in European elections, and women thus face less competition from men in being selected as candidates.

Women in local government and in administration

Women have been more successful in gaining election in local rather than in national government in Britain, but even here, as Stacey and Price observe, parity is a long way off. In 1969 women formed 12 per cent of successful candidates in local government (Royal Commission for Local Government in England 1969), while the figure for Parliament at the same time was 4.6 per cent. Although local government experience was shown by Currell (1974) to be a factor associated with women gaining candidature at national level, it seems that most women do not get far beyond this stepping stone. (It must be said that most men do not either.)

Activity

Find out how many women and men hold office on committees or as chairpersons on your local parish or county council. How does this compare with the current figures for men and women MPs on page 12? How would you explain any discrepancy with the picture suggested by Stacey and Price?

As Oakley (1981) observes, much decision-making goes on in the various branches of the Civil Service as well as in elected bodies and it is not only at the executive and legislative levels of government that political power is exercised. Despite a 1971 report which led to changes in the rules of employment in the British Civil Service to allow women to pursue careers, marriage, and children simultaneously, and despite the fact

124

that since 1962 women and men in the Civil Service have enjoyed equal pay, women are still grossly underrepresented in higher status positions in the Civil Service. As shown in the table below, they remain concentrated in the lower status positions.

Table 12 *Non-industrial Home Civil Service: male and female staff in post in Open Structure and Administrative Group, 1 January 1980*

	Staff in post % men	% women
Open Structure (excl. Parliamentary Counsel)		
Permanent secretary	100	0
Deputy secretary	97.5	2.5
Under secretary	95.6	4.4
Administrative Group		
Assistant secretary	94.3	5.7
Senior principal	97.5	2.5
Principal	92.2	7.8
Senior executive officer	92.5	7.5
Higher executive officer (A)	71.1	28.9
Higher executive officer	83.5	16.5
Executive officer	62.4	37.6
Clerical officer	34.1	65.9
Clerical assistant	20.0	80.0

Source: Civil Service Department *Civil Service Statistics, 1980*, Table 4. (Crown copyright; reproduced with the permission of the Controller of HMSO.)

Voting patterns and political interest

There is clearly an enormous discrepancy between possession and use of the vote by women, and the exercise of political power by women at high levels within the political system. Dowse and Hughes (1972) tell us that one of the best

researched findings in British politics is that women participate less, and are less interested in politics, than men. Women
are more likely to abstain than men, and when they do vote,
are more likely to vote Conservative. The idea that women are
somehow less interested in politics than men has been
vigorously challenged by feminists in recent years. Delamont
(1980) claims that most adults (*both* men and women) are not
active or especially interested in politics, except to vote in
national elections and to identify in a somewhat vague
fashion with the image of a particular party. Goot and Reid
(1975) accuse most political scientists of ignoring gender as a
variable and of carrying out research into 'political interest' in
a highly sexist manner. They argue that it is only accurate to
describe women as less interested than men in politics if one
uses a narrow definition of 'politics', as many researchers
have. Butler and Stokes (1971), for example, in their attempts
to find out how important certain issues were to voters and
what voters' attitudes were, asked their sample about a
number of specific issues including class, the Royal Family,
comprehensive schools, the police, and BBC television.
However, their list did not include any of the issues on which
women's campaigns had focused in recent years, such as equal
pay, abortion, or the management of pregnancy and childbirth.
Had it done so, the results of the research might have been
quite different. Delamont (1980) comments that researchers
have nearly always defined 'politics' in terms of male interests.
Therefore those areas that particularly affect women, such as
childcare and family benefits are, by implication, non-political.

Goot and Reid maintain that such findings that children are
influenced by their father's politics, that women are politically
conservative, and that women constantly change their political
allegiance, are all findings that rest on dubious assumptions
and are not supported by hard data. The literature also
contains many contradictory statements about women: for
example, they are described as both conservative and as
changing their political views in an irrational way. They claim
the greater conservatism of women has been exaggerated and

over-simplified: women's understanding of their social class position may not be the same as those definitions used in the bulk of the research, which usually classify women on the basis of their husband's occupation or that of the male head of the household.This may not be the class to which the woman feels she belongs, nor the one in which her own occupation would place her. The relationship between class and political party may not be the same for women as it is for men. They also argue that there is no basis for accepting the idea that women are influenced by their husband's political views. None of the research quoted in support of this idea actually studied husbands and wives as married couples; it interviewed married men in some households and married women in others. Most of the interviewers used were female, and Goot and Reid argue that this would have seriously influenced the answers given by male respondents, who would be less likely to admit to a female interviewer that their wives had independent, perhaps conflicting political views to their own. Delamont (1980) sums up her discussion of this whole area by saying that what is even more important than more research into the subject of women's attitudes is a change in attitude on the part of researchers. Women must be viewed, not with prejudice, but dispassionately: they must be treated as rational, classified into social classes by their own occupation, and their political activities should be recognized and acknowledged.

History of women's political activity

The traditional, family-centred conservative apolitical woman is as much of a myth today as she was in the past, argues Delamont. Feminist historians and others have provided many rich illustrations of women's participation in political activities in the past. The history of the movement for female suffrage is probably the most famous example of this, but all too often it is the only example of political action by women in the past of which people are aware. Less well-known is the participation of women in food riots in the eighteenth and nineteenth centuries in Britain, and their role in other campaigns, for instance those of the Chartists in the 1830s and in the Temperance Movement in both Britain and the USA in the 1880–90s. Oakley comments that 'women's participation in trade union and radical politics in the nineteenth and early twentieth century [in Britain] was absolutely crucial to the development of the modern Labour party' (1981).

Activity

Consult history textbooks in order to find out more about the political activities of the following: Eleanor Marx, Annie Besant, Mary Astell, Frances Willard, the Woman's Labour League 1906–18.

You may need to consult a book like *Spare Rib Reader* edited by Marsha Rowe (1982), published by Penguin, to gain this information, or read an article like 'Women and Nineteenth Century Radical Politics' in *The Rights and Wrongs of Women* edited by Mitchell and Oakley (1976). If standard history textbooks do not have the information, why do you think this is?

As Thompson (1976) notes, since the 1850s there has been a gradual disappearance of working-class women from radical political activity in Britain; the suffragettes were mainly middle class. Thompson suggests that the 'modernization of working class politics', through the development of structured political groups such as trade unions, pressure groups, and co-operative societies, was a factor in this. Women's lifestyles did not easily allow their participation in such forms, which demanded regularity in working times and income. Also, among women themselves at this time, there was a change in expectations about their place in society; they seem to have accepted a self-image involving 'home centredness and inferiority'. People's acceptance of the patriarchal family combined with this, led to a decline in working-class women's participation in politics.

The re-emergence of the Women's Liberation Movement

The Women's Liberation Movement which resurfaced in western societies in the 60s is very much a middle-class movement, according to Mitchell (1971) and others. The aims of this movement might be described as follows: the creation of awareness among women of the inequalities they have experienced in the past and which they currently experience; the securing of rights for women as individuals in all areas of social life; the improvement of women's self-image. However, the label 'Women's Liberation Movement' may be misleading in that it suggests a coherence and unity that does not actually exist within the movement. There is no one organization, leader, or ideological position which completely represents all the women who feel they are part of this movement; in no sense is the women's movement something which is formally organized or in which consensus exists about issues. Bouchier prefers the term 'feminist movement', which he defines as 'any form of opposition to any form of social, personal or economic discrimination which women suffer because of their sex' (1983). This term, he says, covers the whole range of feminist beliefs and activities from the most moderate to the most radical.

The women's movement in the 60s had its roots in earlier protests and campaigns involving women. In the USA, for example, middle-class women had been active in the anti-slavery movement in the 1800s. Within it, efforts were often made to prevent them from speaking in public because they were women, and they were virtually excluded from the World Anti-Slavery Convention in London in 1840. This must have led American women to the realization that their own social position was in some ways similar to that of the slaves on whose behalf they were campaigning. Feminism as a radical protest began in the USA in a formal manner in 1848 with a convention at Seneca Falls, which published an alternative Declaration of Independence calling for such reforms as property rights for married women and greater access to education. American feminists came to speak in Britain, but as Bouchier (1983) comments, the contradictions in women's lives were less keenly felt in Britain and this was reflected in a later start for British feminism, a smaller scale organization and a less militant tone in the early days.

In the 1960s the feminist movement once again gathered force in the USA. The background to its re-emergence at this time was found in social protest from black people, students, and youth in general. As in other western societies, there had been an expansion in further and higher education, which meant that more young people were able to develop critical views of society in an atmosphere unrelated to work for economic survival. Also, writes Mitchell (1971), in the USA there was a distinct cult of the individual which discouraged conformity and encouraged questioning. There had also been a large increase in the number of women in the labour market, but despite this and a rise in the level of their education, there was no increase in real career opportunities. In 1963 Friedan's book *The Feminine Mystique* was published: this was a discussion of the sharp differences between the image and reality of the housewife's role, which demonstrated that the 'contented, happy housewife' was a destructive myth. The book had sold over 1 million copies by 1970 and was responsible for initiating the first public discussion of this issue since the 20s. In 1966 Friedan and others started NOW (the National Organisation for Women) 'to take action to bring women into full partnership in the mainstream of US society *now*, exercising all the privileges and responsibilities thereof in truly equal partnership with men.' It welcomed serious male support. NOW organized national demonstrations and conferences – today its membership of over 175,000 makes it the world's largest feminist organization. Its aims were in the reformist, liberal tradition rather than in the radical tradition of smaller groups like the Redstockings, whose aims were to raise women's consciousness and to alter social structures in favour of women, but without the participation of men.

The women's movement in Britain

According to Bouchier (1983), the feminist movement in Britain in the 1960s was a revolutionary movement which posed its challenge in explicitly Socialist or Marxist terms. The women involved, as in the USA, were mainly young graduates or students who were active in politics. Women began to meet in small groups in towns and on campuses to discuss their situation as women – there was no one event or publication which inspired this. The first national gathering of many groups was in Oxford in 1970; here it was agreed to bypass the conventional forms of party and pressure group politics in favour of a movement operating outside the system. The conference established the first four demands of the feminist movement – equal pay for equal work, equal opportunities and education, free contraception and abortion on demand, and free 24-hour childcare. The first demonstration in support of these demands was held in London in 1971. The movement grew and expanded without any formal structures or systems of communication. A typical group in the 1970s would consist of about twelve members who rarely talked about issues with other groups.

Activity

An important means of spreading ideas in the feminist movement was and is via journals and magazines. Obtain back copies of some of the following British magazines from a library to find out which issues most concerned feminists in the 70s: *Shrew, Socialist Woman, Red Rag, Sappho, Spare*

Rib. (A polytechnic, university, or further education college library should be able to help.)

Obtain a current issue of *Spare Rib* (now on sale at most newsagents) and compare and contrast it with a popular woman's magazine like *Woman's Own*. Look at the subject and style of advertisements, the subject matter of features and stories, and the sex of the writers. You could pool your results in a group discussion.

Consciousness raising and women's groups

Consciousness raising implies the creation of an awareness among women of their common situation in society and an awareness that what they experience as private problems is the result of the way that social structures oppress women. It was, and is, a central aim of the feminist movement. Discussion usually takes place in small groups. The topics Philpott (1982) discussed in her group included families, friends, childhood, colleagues, lovers, painful experiences, dreams, fears, secrets, future plans. She writes:

'We [the women in the group] were continually surprised, encouraged and excited by the similarity of our experiences, and as this sharing went on many of us found the confidence to do things that really mattered to us, however trivial. We were able to make important personal changes, in both self-image and lifestyle; decisions which we had previously avoided or ignored. Through consciousness raising there is the realisation that you are no longer alone. What you are voicing is no longer anger at yourself and what you took to be personal failings, but rather at society which continues to oppress us all as women.'

The group she belonged to kept to a written agenda and produced a newsletter as well as organizing outings.

Some women's groups set up women's centres in their areas which were open to women for meetings, workshops, playgroups, and campaign projects. By 1973 there were five such centres in London and others, some financed by local authority grants, in other cities. In 1971 a centre in Chiswick became specifically a centre for battered women and others followed. The first rape crisis centre, offering support and advice to victims, was set up in 1976, and today there are many more of these. Members of women's groups of various kinds spoke in schools, colleges, at trades union meetings, and at women's institute meetings. Many local campaigns were organized – for example, the Belsize Women's Group successfully protested against a ruling from a Wimpy bar not to serve unaccompanied women after 11.00 pm – and women also organized play schemes for children and made feminist films, some through the Feminist Film Workshop. Some small groups were set up in schools. Nine girls from a comprehensive school wrote an account of doing this for *Spare Rib*, in which they comment: 'There is really no school with girls and women in it which doesn't need a women's group.'

Campaigns of the women's movement

Campaigns and demonstrations of various kinds were and are an important part of the feminist movement in all western societies. One of the first public demonstrations by women in this country was the disruption of the annual Miss World beauty contest in 1970 by about 100 women. The major campaigns of the early 70s were on abortion and sexual liberation as well as the pursuit of economic demands mainly in relation to working-class women. The latter involved campaigning on such issues as equal pay, unionization of exploited women (such as the night cleaners campaign), financial and legal independence for married women in pensions schemes and state benefits. The wages for housework campaign (see also page 57) was initiated in 1975. In 1974 feminists and trades unionists together produced the Working Women's Charter, a 10 point charter which included demands on maternity leave, family allowances, promotion, and wages. Later, there were campaigns for the proper enforcement of the Equal Pay and Sex Discrimination Acts.

Abortion in Britain was legalized on certain grounds in 1967 and the aim of feminists was to extend these to allow free abortion on demand. The key slogan of this campaign was 'A woman's right to choose'. The National Abortion Campaign, the umbrella group of this campaign, led a number of protests against private member's bills introduced in the Commons which were designed to restrict the grounds on which abortion was available. Finally, one of the major topics for discussion in the movement was sexuality and specifically the nature of female sexuality and sexual relationships between women. Almost all feminist groups have supported the right of gay people of both sexes to express their sexuality openly, but there has been less support for the more recent claim that lesbianism is an intrinsic or central aspect of feminism and that the way forward for the movement lies in the social, political, and sexual separation of women from men. In 1979 a paper was published from a Leeds Revolutionary Feminist Group which spoke in support of lesbianism:

'We do think all feminists can and should be political lesbians . . . it does not mean compulsory sexual activity with women . . . any woman who takes part in a heterosexual couple helps to shore up male supremacy by making its foundations stronger.'

The Leeds group were stating that women could not win their fight against male domination while engaging in sexual relationships with men – change in society to benefit women could only be achieved by women separating and dissociating themselves from men. There continues to be a debate on this issue notably in relation to the anti-nuclear protest at Greenham Common which is for women only. Other campaigns included protests about pornography and male violence towards women (notably the 'reclaim the night' demonstrations in the late 70s).

Activity

Find out, either from a feminist magazine like *Spare Rib* or by contacting one of the relevant organizations, what kinds of campaign are currently being organized on such issues as abortion, pornography, prostitution, and health. Find out also what kinds of campaign black women are organizing within the movement.

Examples of organizations you might contact are: WAR (Women Against Rape), WAVAW (Women Against Violence Against Women), PLAN (Prostitution Laws Are Nonsense), Women Against Racism and Fascism, A Woman's Right to Work. Addresses are found in *Spare Rib* magazine.

In 1978 a national conference established a list of seven demands of the women's movement – a list which has not been altered. These demands are: equal pay for equal work, equal opportunity and equal education, free contraception and abortion on demand, free community-controlled child-care, legal and financial independence for all women, an end to discrimination against lesbians, freedom for all women from intimidation by the threat or use of violence or sexual coercion, regardless of marital status, an end to all laws, assumptions, and institutions that perpetuate male dominance and men's aggression towards women. Not all feminists agree with these demands, nor do they think that all of them are achievable without a revolution. Within the movement there are campaigns on issues not covered by the list – for example, racism, wages for housework, the movement for home births – and debates on such subjects as motherhood and non-sexist child rearing. The women's movement is, as Bouchier puts it, 'very much alive' in the 80s.

135

Hostile attitudes towards the feminist movement on the part of men and women are common. Some newspapers have ridiculed the women involved and trivialized the campaigns they have organized: feminists have been described in the press as 'bra burners' and 'women's libbers'. Bouchier (1983) writes that feminism has been made a scapegoat for many social changes which people find disturbing, such as rising divorce rates, increasing competition from women in the labour market, the greater stresses of family life, or the greater autonomy women as individuals now have. There is a widely accepted view that feminism has spoiled a relationship between men and women which was previously happy and stable.

Many women are indifferent or opposed to feminism. Those women who enjoy a 'traditional female role' within society see it as a threat, while the focus on certain issues within the movement, such as lesbianism and abortion, strikes some women as morally or personally repugnant. Among some women the response takes the form of an increased stress on traditional femininity as the 'correct' role for women, shown by female characters in such television soap operas as 'Dallas' and 'Dynasty'. Some women have become involved in organized groups campaigning against some reforms proposed by feminists, as for example SPUC (Society for the Protection of the Unborn Child) which has branches all over the country, and LIFE, an anti-abortion group which offers practical support to women with unwanted pregnancies and uses the slogan 'a woman's right to kill' to describe the proposals of those who would liberalize abortion law.

Men have not been universally hostile to the feminist movement. Some men have worked with such groups as NAC and others have become involved in men's anti-sexist groups. However, as Bouchier writes (1983)

'it runs counter to centuries of history for men to accept the idea of undifferentiated, androgynous sex roles . . . nobody

136

need be surprised that when women try to move into male spheres of power and influence most men react with hostility'.

The roots of men's hostility towards feminism, he argues, lie far deeper than in the mere defence of male interests – they reflect centuries of socialization of value systems according to which women have been repressed because they have been seen as dangerous, or as agents of chaos. Men fear female biology because they cannot control or understand it; and some feminists have produced (perhaps understandably) a hostile reaction from men with declarations to the effect that *all* men are rapists, violent, and obsessed by sex. This is as much a stereotyped and inaccurate view as the view that *all* women are instinctively submissive or maternal. Bouchier says that overall, the record of men as supporters of feminism is 'dismal'. He cites evidence from the 1980 British conference on 'The Women's Liberation Movement and Men' which suggests that 'male feminists' have had a divisive effect on the movement as a whole. As academics they have tried to take over women's studies courses; in politics they have exploited class divisions among women and have tried to challenge the right of women to an autonomous movement.

The future of the women's movement

In many of the societies where the women's movement resurfaced in the 60s, women have gained rights in areas which would once have been unthinkable. In Britain women can no longer be dismissed from a job because they are pregnant and they have the right to maternity leave; in Italy, a Catholic country, women have rights to divorce, equal pay, and abortion under certain circumstances. France has a government minister for women's rights, and in 1981 the EEC published a plan for a community-wide campaign against discrimination. The women's movement has undoubtedly played a part in bringing this about. In the future, writes

137

Bouchier (1983, referring to Britain), whatever the exact form taken by the movement, it will of necessity have adapted to a period very different in character from the 60s – people in the 80s, according to a recent survey in *New Society*, are more conservative, less sceptical, and less likely to rebel, in the context of a harsher economic climate. Wilson (1980) argues that there are ambiguities in the feminist movement which must be resolved. She writes:

> 'What sort of power do [feminists] seek? In what way do we wish to make our mark on the world? Do we want to share in the world or do we simply want 'women's sphere' to be given greater value? Or do we want to break out of these dichotomies altogether?'

Stacey and Price (1981) write that if women really wish to make changes in the societies they live in, they must seek and achieve power positions: 'It is essential that women should enter the political arena since the societies are all male-dominated, for men certainly cannot be relied upon to initiate or carry through the necessary changes.'

Further Reading

A useful follow up here would be Stacey and Price (1981). Bouchier (1983) provides a detailed account of feminism in both Britain and the USA.

7

Gender, crime, and deviance

This chapter begins by illustrating and discussing the different patterns of male and female involvement in crime. Criminal statistics show that, in general, women commit fewer crimes than men. A distinction may be made between those theorists like Box (1983) who, accepting the statistics as valid, offer explanations on why women are less involved in crime than men, and those like Pollak (1961), who argue that women's underrepresentation in crime statistics is a social construct, resulting from the actions of such authorities as police officers and judges. A related, but separate issue, is that of 'male' and 'female' crimes. Most of the chapter deals with women and girls rather than with men and boys. Traditional criminology has concerned itself primarily with the male offender, and is to be the subject of another book in this series. What follows is an account of recent attempts to explain the largely neglected areas of female crime and deviance.

Women and crime

In all countries where official statistics are available, the figures show that women commit less crime than men. Leonard (1982) shows that in the USA, although the percentage of women arrested for all crimes has increased in recent years, women still only constitute 15.7 per cent of all arrests and only 19.5 per cent of arrests for serious offences such as homicide and robbery with violence. The only crimes for which female arrests exceed male arrests are prostitution and running away from home (for adolescents), and in every other category females constitute less than one-quarter of all arrests. Leonard claims that statistics show virtually no change over time in female involvement in violent crime. There is a considerable discrepancy between the number of offences committed by women and the number of women imprisoned, according to Simon (1975), who found that 18 out of every 100 arrests in the USA were female, but only 3 out of every 100 sentenced to prison were female. Black women have higher rates of imprisonment and conviction than white women, and working-class women have higher rates than middle-class women.

A similar picture is given by Smart (1976) for Britain. Shoplifting, prostitution, and promiscuity and 'ungovernability' in adolescents are the only offences which British statistics reveal to be predominantly female offences. Many offences in which women are involved are related to the female gender role – for example, offences against children and infants, procuring an illegal abortion, and social security offences. Women in our culture bear most of the responsibility for childcare, with all its stresses; the burden of restricted access to legal abortion falls mainly on women who must ultimately give birth; while with social security offences, Smart argues that legislation is punitive towards unsupported women who have been deserted, widowed, or who are not married. The law assumes that a man who is living with a woman is supporting her financially, whether or not he actually is. Women claimants may attempt to claim more than they are legally entitled to especially if they are 'cohabiting' with a man. Smart comments: 'In this case, their involvement with crime is mainly related to the state's reinforcement of their economically dependent position in society and their role of provider for the children and the home.'

Studies of violent crime, especially homicide, suggest that although women are infrequently involved in these crimes, when a woman is involved the manner of the crime and the choice of victim fit in with a 'feminine' stereotype. Wolfgang (1958) showed that women typically murder their husbands, lovers, or other relatives, while men more often murder close friends or strangers. Women are far less likely than men to beat a victim to death or use excessive violence: typically they use knives or household implements as murder weapons and tend to kill their victims in the kitchen or elsewhere in their own homes. Wolfgang argued that women often murder in anger or self-defence so that the victim is frequently the original aggressor. Ward *et al.* (1969) found that 42 per cent of the victims of females were unable to defend themselves at the time of their death – many of these were asleep or drunk – suggesting that women typically wait for a moment when they are likely to be successful in murder, rather than taking on a conscious, alert, and possibly stronger opponent.

Smart's analysis (1976) distinguishes between 'sex-related offences' (crimes which may be committed by either sex but in practice appear to be committed more by one sex than the other) and 'sex-specific offences' (crimes where members of one sex are actually excluded by the legal definition). In Britain, where the law is generally held to be equally applicable to everyone regardless of sex, race, class, and other distinctions, there are few sex-specific offences. Two exceptions are infanticide, which can only be committed by women 'when the balance of a woman's mind is disturbed by reason of her not having fully recovered from the effects of giving birth to a child', and prostitution. Although male prostitutes are recognized, men are not in practice charged with 'offence by prostitute', which relates to soliciting. When male prostitution does appear in the statistics it is included with non-prostitutive homosexual offences like importuning or indecency between males. The legal definition of prostitution in the USA, although showing some variation between states, is typically sex-specific.

Interpretations of criminal statistics

Pollak (1961) argues that the sex differentials shown in crime statistics are 'mythical'. He maintains that women commit as many crimes as men, but that their crimes remain unreported, as a result of which female crime is masked by its relative invisibility. Pollak claims that women are more able than men to conceal the extent of their criminality because of their position in society. As mothers and child carers, for example, they have much opportunity to neglect or ill treat their children, but such criminal behaviour is difficult to detect because it typically takes place in the privacy of the home, because the victims are highly unlikely to complain, and because the 'revered status of the Mother' means that the public is unlikely to suspect the mother of such action. In the last twenty years a number of studies, using self-reporting techniques and victimization surveys, have tried to challenge Pollak's claim that the massive extent of 'invisible' female crime can never be accurately measured. These studies indicate that there are real differences in male and female criminal behaviour, and as a result of them, writes Box (1983), 'Pollak's image of the 'masked female offender' is fast being turned into a myth.' It is now generally accepted among criminologists that official criminal statistics point to real differences as far as male and female crime is concerned.

Does a 'chivalry factor' exist?

Some writers, including Pollak, argue that criminal statistics are distorted with respect to gender because women are

142

treated more leniently than men. According to this view, the police and judiciary are protective, or chivalrous, towards women because of the stereotyped ideas they hold about women. They may believe that women are not 'really' criminal because women are by nature gentle and passive, or that it would be morally wrong – indeed, unmasculine – to impose pain and hardship on a member of the 'weaker' sex in the form of an arrest, trial, or prison sentence. Feminists object to such essentialist (see page 7) and paternalistic attitudes, because neither accepts women as individuals in their own right, or as people who are capable of making their own decisions.

There has been much research to discover whether women actually do get more lenient treatment than men, and to discover whether it is the actual offence itself, or the gender of the offender, which most strongly affects treatment and sentencing. Swigert and Farrell (1976), in their US study, argued that decisions to grant bail, to allow trial by jury, to convict, and to imprison, were all influenced by the idea of the 'normal' criminal whose essential characteristic was maleness. Women offenders, who did not correspond to this picture, were treated more leniently throughout the judicial process, and criminal statistics therefore 'reflect the failure of officials to perceive and label females involved in crime'. Box (1983) argues, however, that the majority of the research does not give clear support to the view that women receive more lenient treatment from law enforcement officers. Gregory (1983), Leonard (1982) and other feminists maintain that the 'chivalry factor' is a myth. If it operates at all, it does so very unevenly and mainly in favour of white middle-class women. They claim that women offenders often receive harsher treatment than males. They identify a tendency among the police and other figures in the judicial process to sexualize female offences and to see young women in particular as being in need of moral guidance. When a woman's offence indicates 'inappropriate gender role behaviour', the outcome of interaction with officials, especially the penal outcome, tends to be more severe. The police and courts thus act to protect 'conventional' women by punishing those who do not conform.

A large amount of research on juvenile offenders supports the view that females receive harsher treatment than males for the same type of offence. Chesney Lind (1973), Terry (1970) and Shacklady Smith (1978) all point out that young women are far more likely to be placed in institutions, and therefore appear more criminal, than young men whose criminal/delinquent behaviour is similar. Girls are thought of as requiring more 'protection' from moral danger than boys. A large number of these young girls have not committed any specific offence, but have merely been judged by parents or teachers as 'ungovernable' or 'in need of care and control'. Datesman and Scarpitti (1977) write: 'In the final analysis, the juvenile court appears to be less concerned with the protection of female offenders than with the protection of the sexual status quo.'

Smart (1976) points to the fact that police officers, probation officers, and judges are all able to exercise a certain amount of discretion over the way in which they treat offenders or the kinds of sentence they impose. Smart maintains that such officials are very likely to be influenced by 'common sense' ideas about females and female criminality. They will have come across the idea that females are vulnerable and in need of protection; also, they will have encountered the traditional double standard of morality according to which males are allowed to express their sexuality more openly and freely than females. Smart argues that female offenders are at a disadvantage where sexual offences are concerned because they are likely to be treated more harshly than males.

Women in prison

In several studies of women in penal institutions it has been argued that imprisonment is inappropriate for female offenders;

144

women suffer more hardship in prison than men because while they are there they are deprived of family life and are separated from their children. Carlen (1983) suggests that many women in prison are there for trivial offences and the reason most of them are in custody is because they have behaved inappropriately, as far as the 'traditional' female gender role is concerned. Carlen and Smart argue that the chief role of prisons is actually to resocialize such 'deviant' women and the regimes of most prisons act to reinforce traditional gender roles. Inmates are encouraged to learn 'feminine' skills such as cooking and sewing. Women prisoners have fewer opportunities than male prisoners to benefit from vocational training or to gain qualifications. Hall Williams (1970) found that prison authorities did not see it as either necessary or desirable to offer women prisoners training for semi-skilled jobs, either because the women were seen as incapable of benefiting from such training or because such training was seen as 'irrelevant' to the woman's future role upon release, which was assumed to be that of homemaker rather than wage earner. Smart (1976) suggests that among prison authorities there is a widely held attitude that a woman who accepts her 'feminine' role and who is passive and caring, is also likely to be non-criminal. Richardson's study of an approved school (1969) (now called community homes) showed that adolescent girls were expected to be 'feminine' in relation to their domestic role, but not in relation to their sexual role. This fits in with the widely held notion in our society that 'nice' – non-criminal – girls aren't sexual.

Many penal institutions for women appear to be based on the assumption, common among the classic/early studies of female criminals, that the female criminal is abnormal or pathological, and this is reflected in the way they are run. At Holloway women's prison in London treatment involves therapy, counselling, and often drugs; it is administered by nurses and doctors as well as prison officers. Smart (1976) describes Holloway as having undergone a transformation from a prison into a psychiatric hospital whose purpose is to cure women who are 'sick'.

Why do women commit crime?

How may female crime be explained? Lombroso and Ferrero (1895) offered one of the earliest explanations, based on the concepts of atavism and social Darwinism. Atavism involves the view that all criminal, anti-social individuals are biological throwbacks to an earlier evolutionary stage in human development; social Darwinism refers to the idea that individuals or groups can develop specific psychological or physiological characteristics to help them function more efficiently in their predetermined roles in society. Lombroso and Ferrero studied pictures of convicted female criminals, taking notes of skull measurements, tattoos, and numbers of moles in order to identify signs of atavism. They explained the absence of such signs in terms of the fact that women are less evolved than men and so show fewer visible signs of degeneration. Women's confinement to the home and family was the reason for this lack of evolutionary development. Lombroso and Ferrero argued that women were thus 'naturally' less inclined to crime than men, but the 'born female criminal' was believed to have all the criminal qualities of the male plus all the 'worst' characteristics of women — cunning, deceitfulness, and spite. Such women criminals were also held to be unnatural because they lacked any maternal instinct. The 'true' nature of women was thus presented as antithetical to crime, and women criminals not only as 'abnormal', but as resembling males.

Smart comments:

'Variations on the belief in biological determinism, both of crime and the nature of women; on sexist beliefs in the inferiority of women, and an implicit support of the double standards of morality, along with the failure to take account of the socio-economic, political and legal context

146

in which 'crime' occurs, all appear in later works on female criminals.' (1976)

Thus although Lombroso and Ferrero's work is now viewed by many as intellectually inadequate, its influence remains. This influence can be seen in the theories of W. I. Thomas (1907), who maintained that clear cut biological differences between the sexes can explain their different patterns of crime. It is women's genetically based, deep seated need to give and to receive affection that leads them into crime, particularly for sexual offences like prostitution. Thomas believed that prostitutes were merely doing what all women do – looking for love – but were doing so in a way that is not socially approved. He saw all female crime as primarily sexual. The reason for this criminal behaviour was the erosion of 'traditional' restraints on women who at one time would not have thought of working outside the home or marrying out of their social group. His solution to this was the imposition on all people of a single 'moral standard' in relation to family life, which involved women in a gender role centred on the family.

Pollak (1961), while not relying solely on biology to explain female crime, does claim that there is a biological basis to female criminality, and also views women in a stereotyped fashion. He argues that women inspire men to commit crime and benefit from this while avoiding arrest themselves. Women are presented as possessing great power and cunning which they frequently use for evil purposes; women are described as 'naturally' more deceitful than men. The source of this is the passive role women assume during sexual intercourse (a role which he believes is biologically rather than culturally determined), during which they learn that it is relatively easy to deceive their partner into believing that they are aroused and have had an orgasm. Menstruation, pregnancy, and the menopause are examples of 'psychological disturbances' which may upset the 'need and satisfaction balance of an individual or weaken her internal inhibitions'

147

and thus are potentially causative factors of crime.

Smart (1976) offers a detailed critique of the above studies from a feminist perspective. She comments that, in comparison with the vast amount of work on all aspects of male delinquency and criminality, the amount of research on women and crime is extremely limited. As a result, our knowledge of the nature of female criminality 'is still in its infancy.' She accounts for the lack of research in terms of criminology being a policy-oriented and male-dominated subject. Female criminality has not been viewed as a serious threat to the social order and has not therefore been seen as a worthwhile subject for study. Criminologists have also uncritically accepted commonsense and stereotyped views of women as 'inferior' and 'different'. The result is that female criminality and deviance have been presented as derived from biological or psychological factors peculiar to females.

Why do women commit so few serious crimes?

Some feminists, like Leonard (1982), and Smart (1976), argue that traditional criminology has not satisfactorily explained female crime, and that a special theory of female criminality is necessary. Traditional criminology, they maintain, is male-biased: it has been constructed by men, and its subject is men. They claim that an explanation for female crime can be found in gender role socialization and in forms of male domination of society. Female criminality is relatively rare because the gender socialization of females into passive, conforming, and subordinate roles is so successful. Smart states that a particularly important aspect of the socialization of girls is the restrictions placed on their freedom of movement at an age when most boys are 'discovering' delinquency – namely adolescence (see also page 18). The ability of girls to participate in criminality is structurally restricted – they lack access to 'illegitimate opportunity structures', or opportunities to witness, learn about, and become involved in delinquency.

Box (1983) maintains that the sex-differential in crime rates can best be accounted for by the fact that, in comparison with their male peers, adolescent girls are relatively less powerful, and this crucial social difference persists into adulthood. Organized crime, like paid employment, is not an equal opportunity employer: women rarely find themselves in positions where they are free to execute major crimes. Their resources and opportunities simply do not facilitate it; the level of surveillance and social disapproval inhibit it.

Box points out that most research on women and crime in recent years has focused on adolescents who, according to official statistics commit one-third of all serious crimes in England and Wales. There is as yet little real illumination of why adult women commit so few serious crimes in relation to the total committed by men.

Activity

Make a collection of newspaper articles from the national dailies for one week, which deal with crime stories. Count the number of stories in which males and females are the offender and victim respectively. Do your findings fit the picture of male and female crime given in this chapter? What explanations are given for the crime in each case, and do you think there are any obvious differences in attitude expressed by journalists towards offenders and victims of different sexes?

Prostitution

Prostitutes have been the subject of much research, but as McIntosh (1978) has shown, most of this work has been heavily influenced by stereotyped beliefs about prostitutes. Lombroso and Ferrero (1895) saw prostitution as a major sign of degeneracy and recently prostitutes have been described as women who are immature, lesbian, coming from broken

149

homes, sick, or not responsible for their own actions, as Delamont (1980) has commented. Many studies accept the legal definition of 'prostitution', which takes the view that it is a social evil requiring remedy; and few of these studies have presented prostitutes as rational individuals capable of making their own decisions. Few studies make reference to a possible economic explanation for prostitution. Prostitution may be partly a reflection of the fairly limited opportunities for women in advanced industrial societies to earn a good wage, to be economically independent, and to be financially secure. It may have its attractions for women who are economically dependent, either on men or on the welfare state, especially since a woman can often earn far more in prostitution than in many 'legitimate' kinds of work.

Smart (1976) compares prostitutes and wives in order to illustrate the point that the act of exchanging sexual favours for economic reward is not always viewed as deviant or illegal. The main difference between a wife's and a prostitute's sexual relationships, she states, is that those of the former take place within marriage and involve one man, while those of the latter take place outside marriage with a number of men. The law on prostitution is another example of law which punishes those women whose behaviour implicitly challenges the 'moral rightness' of the family institution and the traditional female role of dependence within it. Smart argues that, in their concentration on female prostitution, neglect of male prostitution and of prostitutes' clients, and dependence on a pathological model and acceptance of 'traditional' gender roles, no study of prostitution carried out so far meets even the basic requirements of a feminist perspective.

Rape

Rape legislation

Rape is defined by the law in highly specific terms in western societies as the act of the penis penetrating the vagina without the consent of the woman concerned. In Britain, most European countries, and in over forty states in the USA there is what Box (1983) calls a 'spousal exception' clause in rape laws: a married woman cannot be raped by her husband. This is one reason why feminists and others have protested against rape laws in these societies over the last ten years. They see the law as endorsing the notion that wives are their husbands' property rather than being individuals in their own right. Feminists object to rape law for other reasons as well: first, they claim, its notion of 'consent' places an unfair burden of proof on the victim; second, it fails to include consideration for consent obtained by coercion; and third, it reflects a male preoccupation with just *one* of the many ways in which a woman may be violated. Box (1983) writes that because the legal definition of rape is very narrow, 'much behaviour which is very similar in *form*, although not in *content*, is omitted and ignored'. He suggests that those who work within the legal definition of rape will look only for a certain type of violence on the part of the attacker to prove that intercourse occurred without the woman's consent. Women may sometimes be coerced by 'economic, emotional and social' as well as physical violence, he argues: a woman may be threatened by job loss, demotion, transfer to an unpleasant job location, loss of affection, or the promise of marriage being withdrawn; she may be threatened by a male who has the power to stigmatize her, as when a policeman can offer her non-arrest for herself or a relative in return for sexual favours.

Feminists and others argue for a broader legal definition of rape: as 'sexual access gained by any means where the female's overt, *genuine* consent is absent.'

Popular accounts of rape

Reports of rape cases in the popular press suggest that rape is an isolated, spontaneous act carried out by a man who is disturbed or abnormal. The rapist is often presented as a psychopath who is 'different' from 'normal' men. The popular press does not always treat the victim sympathetically, especially if she is seen as promiscuous or imprudent; she may well be seen as having provoked rape. Smart (1976) states that the stereotyped picture of rape is important because it creates a situation in which it is very difficult for a 'normal' male to imagine that he could be a rapist; the stereotyped view of victims reinforces the idea that rape does not happen to 'normal' respectable women.

Amir (1971) presents a very different view of rapists and rape victims from that given in the popular press. His study of rape in Philadelphia attacks the popular notion of rapists as strangers to their victims. He found that rapist and victim are frequently known to one another, if only by sight, and also that rape most frequently occurs within the rapist's or the victim's home, rather than in the street. Most rapes involved a considerable amount of planning beforehand so that rape is not in reality a 'spontaneous' event. Such studies as the accounts of rape victims by Connell and Wilson (1974) disprove some of the other popular assumptions about rape, namely that women enjoy it; that only young, attractive women are raped; and that a victim's resistance can prevent a rape occurring. Amir also showed that rape was accompanied by violence in over three-quarters of the cases he studied, and this often involved humiliation of the victim. Smart (1976) argues that such evidence can be used to challenge the popular assumption that rape is a method of gaining sexual satisfaction for frustrated men. The very considerable degrees of violence and humiliation involved would suggest that rape is not a purely sexual act: rather, it is the expression of a violent hatred of women, an act of extreme hostility.

Rape is much more widespread than official statistics would suggest. Brownmiller (1975) and others have suggested that the stigma and blame frequently attached to the victim prevent many women from reporting rape to the police in the first place. It is widely believed that the police are un-sympathetic to rape victims, especially if they have been sexually active. Greer (1975) suggests that many rape victims fail to recognize or even recall their own victimization. This is particularly likely to happen in 'seduction-turned-into-rape' cases, where the woman blames herself for the event, thinking that in some way – perhaps by the clothes she wore, or her physical response – she must have consented.

Box (1983) writes that in England and Wales, of the minority of men who are eventually arrested and charged with rape, over one-quarter of these are found 'not guilty' and of the remainder one quarter are not sent to prison.

Understanding rape

Feminists and others argue that rape cannot be understood in isolation from an analysis of the position of women and notions of sexuality operating within a given culture. In western societies, they maintain, rape acts, in conjunction with other forms of aggression against women, as an implicit form of social control on women. Box (1983) writes: 'the stereotypes of men and women in our culture prepare *those who accept them* to place themselves unwarily into a 'rape trap'. Male gender role socialization is a 'cultural precondition of rape' because it reduces women, in men's minds, to sex objects and because it emphasizes men as the initiators of sexual relationships. It also prepares men for strong resistance to their advances. Box writes: 'out of this it is but an easy step to link sex with aggression and assertiveness and hence see rape and seduction as the same sexual act of conquest over a reluctant and coy adversary.'

In our culture 'femininity' involves notions of passivity, submissiveness, and dependence: according to Weis (1975), these elements prepare women to be rape victims. Our culture also teaches women that their sexuality may be used to bargain for male protection and economic support. Smart (1976) writes: 'Rape may be said to be 'normal' given a social context in which male sexuality and aggression are equated and female sexuality is repressed and rendered passive.'

153

Further Reading

Readers may try chapters four (on rape and sexual assaults on females) and five (on female crime) in Box (1983). For an explicitly feminist perspective there is Smart (1976).

Appendix:
Content Analysis

The following general guide may be used by those wishing to carry out content analysis, as suggested in some of the activities in this book.

1 Devise an appropriate list of categories; for an analysis of advertisements for example, these might include 'man washing up', 'man playing with children', 'woman cooking', or 'woman using washing machine'.

2 Count up, in each magazine, book, television programme, or newspaper you are considering, the number of times a photograph or text shows a character or person doing these things.

3 You will then be in a position to identify patterns within a particular book, magazine etc., and to make statistical comparisons between different examples of whatever you have analysed.

4 The final stage is when you attempt to explain any patterns, similarities, or differences you have identified.

References

Adams, C. and Lauriekitis, R. (1976) *The Gender Trap* Volume 1 *Education and Work*, Volume 2 *Sex and Marriage*, Volume 3 *Messages and Images*. London: Virago.

Adams, C. (1982) *Ordinary Lives: A Hundred Years Ago*. London: Virago.

Adelman, C. (1980) In Delamont *The Sociology of Women*. London: George Allen & Unwin.

Alexander, S. (1976) 'Women's Work in Nineteenth Century London'. In Mitchell, J. and Oakley, A. (eds) *The Rights and Wrongs of Women*. Harmondsworth: Penguin.

Amir, M. (1971) *Patterns of Forcible Rape*. Chicago: University of Chicago Press.

Badinter, E. (1980) The Myth of Motherhood – *A Historical View of the Maternal Instinct*. London: Souvenir Press.

Barnes, K. (1970) *He and She*. Harmondsworth: Penguin.

Barron, R. and Norris, G. (1978) 'Sexual Divisions and the Dual Labour Market'. In Barker, D. and Allen, S. (eds) *Dependence and Exploitation in Work and Marriage*. London: Routledge & Kegan Paul.

Belotti, E. (1975) *Little Girls*. London: Writers' & Readers' Publishing Co-operative.

Best, L. and Birke, E. (1980) The Tyrannical Womb: Menstruation and the Menopause. In Brighton Women and Science Group (eds) *Alice Through the Microscope: The Power of Science over Women's Lives*. London: Virago.

Bouchier, D. (1983) *The Feminist Challenge*. London: Macmillan.

Bowlby, J. (1953) *Child Care and the Growth of Love*. Harmondsworth: Pelican.

Box, S. (1983) *Power, Crime, and Mystification*. London: Tavistock.

Braman, O. (1977) Comics. In King, J. and Stott, M. (eds) *Is This Your Life*. London: Virago.

Brighton Women and Science Group (eds) *Alice Through the Microscope: the Power of Science over Women's Lives*. London: Virago.

Brown, D. (1980) *Disruptive Behaviour in a London Comprehensive*. Unpublished.

Brownmiller, S. (1975) *Against Our Will: Men, Women and Rape*. London: Secker and Warburg.

Bruegel, I. (1982) Women as a Reserve Army of Labour: a Note on Recent British Experience. In Whitelegg, E. *The Changing Experience of Women*. Oxford: Martin Robertson.

Butler, D. and Stokes, R. (1971) *Political Change in Britain*. Harmondsworth: Penguin.

Byrne. E. (1978) *Women and Education*. London: Tavistock.

Carlen, P. (1983) *Women's Imprisonment: A Study in Social Control*. London: Routledge.

Chesney Lind, M. (1973) Judicial Enforcement of the Female Sex Role: the Family Court and Female Delinquent. *Issues in Criminology* 8:2.

Clarricoates, C. K. (1978) Dinosaurs in the Classroom: a re-examination of some aspects of the 'hidden curriculum' in primary schools. *Women's Studies International Quarterly* 1:4.

Connell, N. and Wilson, C. (1974) *Rape: the First Sourcebook for Women*. New York: Plume Books.

Conran, S. (1977) *Superwoman*. Harmondsworth: Penguin.

Constantinides, P. (1977) The Greek Cypriots. In Watson, J. (ed.) *Between Two Cultures*. Oxford: Blackwell.

Coussins, J. (1980) Equality for Women: Have the Laws Worked? *Marxism Today*, January.

157

Cowie, C. and Lees, S. (1983) How Boys Slag Off Girls. *New Society*, October.

Currell, M. (1974) *Political Women*. Beckenham: Croom Helm.

Dale, R. (1969) *Mixed or Single-sex School?* London: Routledge & Kegan Paul.

Dalton, K. (1979) *Once a Month*. Claremont: Hunter House.

Datesman, S. and Scarpitti, R. (1977) Unequal Protection for Males and Females in the Juvenile Court. In Ferdinand, T. (ed) *Juvenile Delinquency*. London: Sage.

Davenport. W. (1965) Sexual Patterns and their Regulation in a Society of the South West Pacific. In Beach, F. (ed.) *Sex and Behaviour*. New York: John Wiley.

Davidson, L. and Gordon, S. (1982) *The Sociology of Gender*. Chicago: Rand McNally.

Davie, R., Butler, M., and Goldstein, H. (1972) *From Birth to Seven*. Harlow: Longman.

Deem, R. (1978) *Women and Schooling*. London: Routledge & Kegan Paul.

Delamont, S. (1980) *The Sociology of Women*. London: George Allen & Unwin.

Douglas, J. W. B. (1964) *The Home and the School*. London: MacGibbon & Kee.

Dowse, R. and Hughes, J. (1972) Political Sociology. Chichester: John Wiley.

Durkin, K. and Akhtar, P. (1983) Television, Sex Roles and Children. *New Society*, April.

Ferguson, M. (1983) Learning to be a Woman's Woman. *New Society*, April.

Fletcher, R. (1962) *The Family and Marriage in Britain*. Harmondsworth: Penguin.

Freeman, D. (1983) *Margaret Mead and Samoa: The Making and Unmaking of an Anthropological Myth*. Cambridge: Harvard University Press.

Friedan, B. (1973) *The Feminine Mystique*. Harmondsworth: Penguin.

Gavron, H. (1966) *The Captive Wife*. Harmondsworth: Penguin.

Goodman, L. (1974) A Report on Children's Toys. In Stacey, J., Daniels, J., and Bereaud, J. *And Jill Came Tumbling After*. New York: Dell.

Goot, M. and Reid, E. (1975) *Women and Voting Studies*. London:

Sage.

Gorer, G. (1970) *Sex and Marriage in England Today*. London: Nelson.

Greer, G. (1975) *The Female Eunuch*. St Albans: Paladin.

Gregory, J. (1983) *Sex, Class and Crime*. Middlesex Polytechnic Occasional Paper.

Hall, C. (1982) History of the Housewife. In Rowe, M. (ed.) *Spare Rib Reader*. Harmondsworth: Penguin.

Hall, C. (1982) The Home Turned Upside Down: the Working Class Family in Cotton Textiles 1780–1850. In Whitelegg, E. (ed.) *The Changing Experience of Women*. Oxford: Martin Robertson.

Hall Williams, J. (1970) *The English Penal System in Transition*. London: Butterworth.

Hartley, R. (1966) A Developmental View of Female Sex Role Identification. In Biddle, B. and Thomas, E. (eds) *Role Theory*. Chichester: John Wiley.

Henry, J. (1964) *Jungle People*. St Paul, Minnesota: Vintage Books.

Hills, J. (1981) Participation by Women in the Labour and Conservative Parties. In Stacey, M. and Price, M. *Women, Power, and Politics*. London: Tavistock.

Hobson, D. (1978) Housewives: Isolation as Oppression. In CCCS *Women Take Issue*. London: Hutchinson.

Hope, E. *et al.* (1976) Homeworkers in North London. In Barker, D. and Allen, S. (eds) *Sexual Divisions and Society*. London: Tavistock.

Hunt, A. (1975) *Management Attitudes and Practices Towards Women at Work*. London: HMSO.

Joffe, C. (1971) Sex Role Socialisation and the Nursery School. *Journal of Marriage and the Family* 33:3.

Jolly, H. (1975) *The Book of Child Care*. London: George Allen & Unwin.

Kaberry, P. (1952) *Women of the Grassfields*. London: HMSO.

Kessler, S. and McKenna, W. (1982) Developmental Aspects of Gender. In Whitelegg, E. (ed.) *The Changing Experience of Women*. Oxford: Martin Robertson.

—— (1978) *Gender, An Ethnomethodological Approach*. New York: John Wiley.

Lake (1975) Are we born into our sex roles or programmed into them? *Women's Day*, January.

Land, H. (1975) Myth of the Male Breadwinner. *New Society*,

October.

Leach, P. (1979) *Baby and Child*. Harmondsworth: Penguin.

Leonard, E. (1982) *Women, Crime and Society*. Harlow: Longman.

Lobban, G. (1976) Sex Roles in Reading Schemes. *Educational Review* 27:3.

Lombroso, C. and Ferrero (1895) *The Female Offender*. Fisher Unwin.

Maccoby, E. and Jacklin, C. (eds) (1974) *The Psychology of Sex Differences*. Stanford: University Press.

Malinowski, B. (1963) *The Family Among Australian Aborigines*. New York: Schocken Books.

Mackie, L. and Pattullo, P. (1977) *Women at Work*. London: Tavistock.

Marks, P. (1976) Femininity in the Classroom. In Mitchell, J. and Oakley, A. (eds) *The Rights and Wrongs of Women*. Harmondsworth: Penguin.

Martin, J. and Roberts, C. (1980) *Women and Employment: A Lifetime Perspective*. London: OPCS.

McIntosh, M. (1978) Who Needs Prostitutes? – the Ideology of Male Sexual Needs. In Smart, C. and Smart B., (eds) *Women, Sexuality and Social Control*. London: Routledge & Kegan Paul.

McNeill, P. (1985) Social Science Teacher 14:3.

Mead, M. (1935) *Sex and Temperament in Three Primitive Societies*. New York: William Morrow.

Mellors, C. (1978) *The British MP*. Aldershot: Saxon House.

Millett, K. (1970) *Sexual Politics*. New York: Hart Davis.

Mitchell, J. (1971) *Woman's Estate*. Harmondsworth: Penguin.

Mitchell, J. and Oakley, A. (eds) (1976) *The Rights and Wrongs of Women*. Harmondsworth: Penguin.

Money, J. and Ehrhardt, A. (1972) *Man and Woman, Boy and Girl*. Baltimore: Johns Hopkins Press.

Morris, D. (1967) *The Naked Ape*. London: Jonathan Cape.

Moss, H. (1970) Sex, Age and State as Determinants of Mother–Infant Interaction. In Danziger, K. (ed.) *Readings in Child Socialisation*. Oxford: Pergamon Press.

Moyo, E. (1973) Big Mother and Little Mother in Matabeleland. *New Society*, June.

Murdock, G. (1949) *Social Structure*. London: Macmillan.

Murphy, L. (1962) *The Widening World of Childhood*. New York: Basic Books.

160

Newland, K. (1975) *Women in Politics: a Global Review*. Worldwatch Institute.

Nicholson, J. (1977) *What Society Does to Girls*. London: Virago.

Oakley, A. (1972) *Sex, Gender and Society*. London: Maurice Temple Smith.

—— (1974) *Housewife*. London: Allen Lane.

—— (1981) *From Here To Maternity: Becoming a Mother*. Harmondsworth: Penguin.

—— (1981) *Subject Women*. Harmondsworth: Penguin.

—— (1984) *Taking It Like a Woman*. London: Jonathan Cape.

Parsons, T. (1959) The Social Structure of the Family. In Anshen, R. (ed.) *The Family – Its Function and Destiny*. London: Harper & Row.

Persky, H. *et al.* in Archer, J. and Lloyd, B. (1974) *Sex and Gender*. Harmondsworth: Penguin.

Person, E. (1974) Some New Observations on the Origins of Femininity. In Strouse, J. (ed.) *Women and Analysis*. New York: Grossmann.

Philpott, G. (1982) Consciousness Raising – Back To Basics. In Rowe, M. (ed.) *Spare Rib Reader*. Harmondsworth: Penguin.

Piachaud, D. and Fawcett, H. (1984) *Round About Fifty Hours A Week – the Time Costs of Children*. London: Child Poverty Action Group.

Pollak, O. (1961) *The Criminality of Women*. Philadelphia: University of Pennsylvania Press.

Pollert, A. (1981) *Girls, Wives, Factory Lives*. London: Macmillan.

Radway, J. (1984) *Reading the Romance: Women, Patriarchy and Popular Literature*. Chapel Hill: University of North Carolina Press.

Rance, S. (1982) Going All the Way. In Rowe, M. (ed.) *Spare Rib Reader*. Harmondsworth: Penguin.

Rich, A. (1977) *Of Woman Born*. London: Virago.

Richardson, H. (1969) *Adolescent Girls in Approved Schools*. London: Routledge & Kegan Paul.

Riley, D. (1983) *War in the Nursery*. London: Virago.

Rimmer, L. *et al.* (1980) *Happy Families?* Study Commission on the Family.

Rowbotham, S. (1973) *Woman's Consciousness, Man's World*. Harmondsworth: Penguin.

Rowe, M. (ed.) (1982) *Spare Rib Reader*. Harmondsworth: Penguin.

161

Sayers, J. (1982) *Biological Politics*. London: Tavistock.

Schofield, M. (1965) *The Sexual Behaviour of Young People*. Harmondsworth: Penguin.

Sears, R., Maccoby, E., and Levin, H. (1957) *Patterns of Child-rearing*. London: Harper & Row.

Shacklady Smith, L. (1978) Sexist Assumptions and Female Delinquency. In Smart, C. and Smart, B. (eds) *Women, Sexuality and Control*. London: Routledge & Kegan Paul.

Sharpe, S. (1976) *Just Like a Girl*. Harmondsworth: Penguin

—— (1984) *Double Identity*. Harmondsworth: Penguin.

Simon, R. (1975) *Women and Crime*. Lexington: Lexington Books.

Smart, C. (1976) *Women, Crime and Criminology*. London: Routledge & Kegan Paul.

Smart, C. and Smart, B. (eds) (1978) *Women, Sexuality and Social Control*. London: Routledge & Kegan Paul.

Spare Rib magazine (1978) *Back to School*, October.

Snell, M. (1979) The Equal Pay and Sex Discrimination Acts: Their Impact in the Workplace. *Feminist Review* 1.

Spender, D. (1980) *Man Made Language*. London: Routledge & Kegan Paul.

—— (1982) *Invisible Women: the Schooling Scandal*. London: Writers' & Readers' Publishing Co-operative.

Spock, B. (1946) *Baby and Child Care*. New York: Pocket Books.

Stacey, M. and Price, M. (1981) *Women, Power, and Politics*. London: Tavistock.

Stanworth, M. (1981) *Gender and Schooling*. Women's Research and Resources Centre.

Swigert, V. and Farrell, R. (1976) *Murder, Inequality and the Law*. Lexington: Lexington Books.

Terry, R. (1970) Discrimination in the Handling of Juvenile Offenders by Social Control Agencies. In Garabedian, P. and Gibbons, D. (eds) *Becoming Delinquent*. New York: Aldine Press.

Thom, B. (1980) Women in International Organisations: Room at the Top. The Situation in Some UN Organisations. In Epstein and Coser (eds) *Access to Power – Cross-National Studies of Women and Elites*. London: George Allen & Unwin.

Thomas, W. I. (1907) *Sex and Society*. Little Brown.

Thompson, D. (1976) Women and Nineteenth-century Radical Politics: A Lost Dimension. In Mitchell, J. and Oakley, A. (eds)

The Rights and Wrongs of Women. Harmondsworth: Penguin.

Tiger, L. and Fox, R. (1972) *The Imperial Animal.* London: Secker and Warburg.

Turnbull, C. (1965) *Wayward Servants.* London: Eyre and Spottiswoode.

Walker, K. (1954) *The Physiology of Sex and its Social Implications.* Harmondsworth: Penguin.

Walkerdine, V. (1984) Some Day My Prince Will Come. In McRobbie, A. and Nava, M. (eds) *Gender and Generation.* London: Macmillan.

Wallsgrove, R. (1980) The Masculine Face of Science. In Brighton Women and Science Group (eds) *Alice Through the Microscope: Power of Science over Women's Lives.* London: Virago.

Ward, R., Ward, D. and Jackson, M. (1969) Crimes of Violence by Women. In Mulvihill, D. *et al.* (eds) *Crimes of Violence* Volume 13. Washington: Government Printing Office.

Weeks, J. (1981) *Sex, Politics and Society: The Regulation of Sexuality Since 1800.* Harlow: Longman.

Weis, K., Weis, S. and Borges, S. (1975) Victimology – the Justification of Rape. In Drapkin, I. and Viano, E. (eds) *Victimology: A New Focus – Violence and its Victims.* Lexington: Lexington Books.

Whitelegg, E. (ed.) (1982) *The Changing Experience of Women.* Oxford: Martin Robertson.

Willmott, P. and Young, M. (1962) *Family and Kinship in East London.* Harmondsworth: Penguin.

—— (1975) *The Symmetrical Family.* Harmondsworth: Penguin.

Wilson, D. (1978) Sexual Codes and Conduct. In Smart, C. and Smart, B. (eds) *Women, Sexuality and Social Control.* London: Routledge & Kegan Paul.

Wilson, E. (1980) Beyond the Ghetto: Thoughts on Beyond the Fragments – *Feminism and the Making of Socialism* by Wainwright, H., Rowbotham, S. and Segal, L. *Feminist Review* 4.

Winnicott, D. (1944) Getting to know your baby. *Six Broadcast Talks.* London: BBC. *See also* Riley (1983).

Wolfgang, M. (1958) *Patterns of Criminal Homicide.* Philadelphia: University of Pennsylvania Press.

Wolpe, A. M. (1977) *Some Processes in Sexist Education.* London: Women's Research and Resources Centre.

Index

educational provision for males and females, history of 61–3
employers' attitudes to working women 7, 104, 107, 113
Employment Protection Act 114
Equal Opportunities Commission 115
Equal Pay Act 103, 134
examination results by sex 71–3

Ferguson, M. 31
Fletcher, R. 39
Freeman, D. 12

gender development, theories of 21–5
gender identity 20–1
gender role 20–1
girls' attitudes to education 77
Goodman, M. 28
Goot, M. and Reid, E. 126
government attitudes to working women 113
Greer, G. 33, 153

Hadow Report 62
Hall, C. 47, 97
Hartley, R. 26–7
Henry, J. 17
hidden curriculum 81–2
homeworking 105
housework 27, 40, 41; hours 43; and motherhood 43; in non-western cultures 44–6; history of 47; and the curriculum 61–2; and housewives 42
Hunt, A. 7, 107

industrial action and women 110
industrialization and women's work 97, 98

Kaberry, P. 46
Kessler, W. and McKenna, S. 23, 25

Land, H. 104
language and gender 35, 36
Leonard, E. 140, 143, 148
Lobban, G. 70

Maccoby, E. and Jacklin, C. 24, 26
Malinowski, B. 46
married women workers 99, 100, 115, 116, 148
Martin, J. and Roberts, C. 115, 116
Marxist feminists 32–3; and advertising 34–5; and housework/childcare 57
maternal instinct 51, 53; and crime 146
McIntosh, M. 15, 149
McNeill, P. 72
Mead, M. 11
Mellors, C. 121
Millett, K. 58
Mitchell, J. 59, 129, 130
Money, J. and Ehrhardt, A. 8, 24, 25
Moss, H. 26
mothering in non-western cultures 52
Murdock, G. 5, 11, 56
Murphy, L. 26

Newsom Report 62
nursery schools 65; in wartime 48; and teachers 66, 67

Oakley, A. 7, 9, 11, 16, 17, 28, 41, 42, 48, 53, 57, 100, 102, 107, 112, 121, 124, 128

paid employment: gender divisions 96; and war 48
parents and babies 26; attitudes to girls' and boys' education 75–6
Parsons, T. 6, 51, 56
part-time women workers 99, 104–05; and redundancy 108
Philpott, G. 132
Piachaud, D. and Fawcett, H. 49, 54
Plowden Report 68
politics: and women in government outside Britain 123; and women in Parliament 120–22; and women in local government 124; and women's voting patterns 126–27; and women in international organizations 123; see also women's liberation movement